THE GOOD TIMES
ARE KILLING ME

THE GOOD TIMES ARE KILLING ME

A Novel by
Lynda Barry

HarperPerennial
A Division of HarperCollins*Publishers*

For Mrs. Yvonne Taylor who still lives across the alley, and for Mrs. Claire LaSane who taught me how to read and write.

Cover design by Lynda Barry.
Cover painting: *The Good Times Are Killing Me* © 1988 Lynda Barry, from the collection of Nicole Hollander.
All photographs by Robert Vinnedge.

This book was originally published in 1988 by The Real Comet Press. It is here reprinted by arrangement with The Real Comet Press.

First HarperPerennial edition published 1991.

Designed by Lynda Barry and Ed Marquand Book Design

LIBRARY OF CONGRESS CATALOG CARD NUMBER 91-55107

ISBN 0-06-097424-9

91 92 93 94 95 BVG 10 9 8 7 6 5 4 3 2 1

Contents

Do you ever wonder what is music? Who invented it and what for and all that? And why hearing a certain song can make a whole entire time of your life suddenly just rise up and stick in your brain?

◎ My Street

My name is Edna Arkins. As usual, I'm stuck sitting around watching my sister and my cousin Ellen's baby until my mother gets home from work.

Come over here and look out this window. You see that street? That's my same old street. I know everything that has ever happened on it and everything that is ever going to happen on it. In the beginning of this street it was a mainly white street. That was a long time ago, but I can remember the houses went White, White, White, Japanese, White, White. Across the street and down the next two blocks were about the same except there was more Japaneses, two Chinese and a Philippines house on the corner by the woods. Down Crowley was where all the Negro houses started. Them and some other houses, a white motorcycle house with sheets for curtains and two white trash houses with matching refrigerators laying on their sides in the yards.

Then was the first Negro house ever on our street, the Vidrines of Mrs. Vidrine who worked at our school. They had high school twins named Lillian and Lionel and about five other children who were married and would bring their babies over in cars on Sunday afternoons, which made my Aunt Margaret mad when she came over because she couldn't get her usual parking space.

Then the Quicks moved away, which was fine with us because can you believe they thought *we* wrecked the street when we moved in? Then the Mosely's moved, fine with us too because they thought they were better than everyone just because of their car. And then the Aymond's moved, which was sad because they were so nice and always gave the best candy for Halloween, but they were old and said they had to go live somewhere easier. Then it seemed like just about everybody kept moving out until now our street is Chinese, Negro, Negro, White, Japanese, Filipino, and about the same but in different orders for down the whole street and across the alley.

9

◎ My Song

You know how when people say "They're playing our song"? Or like how the stars have a theme song that plays right before they come out from behind a curtain? Well I had a song too. Probably everybody did. It's the first song you could really sing, the one your parents made you do over and over to show all your relatives how above average you were. And you can't ever change your song. Once a song is yours, it's yours for life.

Mine was by Louis Armstrong who I did one of my reports on recently and found out that he learned to play the trumpet at such an early age by shooting off a gun in the middle of a downtown street on the fourth of July. He got locked up in juvenile for it where there was a music teacher who handed him a trumpet. The book I read on him said that getting put in the Colored Waif's Home was the luckiest thing that ever happened to him because if you want to get professional on an instrument you really do have to concentrate, and it turns out that jail is one of the best places to do it. Later he grew up and played for the Queen of England.

Louis Armstrong's song "What a Wonderful World" was the favorite one of mine, my theme song. When I sang it and did the voice everyone always started laughing and thinking a lot of perfect things about me.

◉ The First Song Of My Life

As far as the first song of my life goes, I think it was "I Went to the Animal Fair" from when I was a baby and the neighbors had told my mother the reason all my hair was falling out was from nerves, and singing me this song might help my condition. My mother must have been pretty worried because I heard the song about forty million times.

Back then, almost all the songs had animals in them doing something. Now, though, there's hardly any animals doing anything in songs. It's just love, love, love, love, love.

The part I remember most went

The big baboon by the light of the moon
Was combing his auburn hair

When I was trying to fall asleep at night, I sometimes would stare at the silver spot of the street light coming through the curtains of our bedroom window and wonder was he trained to do that? And how did his hair get all burned?

My little sister Lucy told me one time that she used to think that street light was in reality God. I don't see how she can even stand to admit that. Nine. You can't get much dumber than when you're nine. She's a lot different than me and it's not just because I'm older. I could always tell the difference between God and a street light.

◎ Borrowing Things

One week when my Uncle Jim and Aunt Margaret were going away on vacation, my dad asked if he could please borrow my uncle's tape recorder to goof around with while they were gone. Dad told him he was thinking of getting one himself one day and just wanted to test out how he would like it. My Uncle Jim is my father's older brother and they haven't liked each other much since when they were little and my dad constantly wrecked things of Jim's—not on purpose—and took away Jim's girlfriends—not on purpose either.

What was Jim going to say when my father asked him right after grace on my dad's combination birthday and Fourth of July dinner, with practically every one of our relatives sitting there to celebrate it? Aunt Margaret looked down at her plate and started making her tiny little faces. My teenager cousin Ellen started doing the same thing because, as you know, monkey see monkey do. Aunt Margaret hated us for owing them so much money, like it was our fault they lent it to us.

"Well I guess I can't see any reason why not," Uncle Jim said after he had tried his hardest to find a reason and just couldn't with everyone staring at him. My father said he would be happy to pick up the tape recorder when he dropped them off at the train station the next Saturday, and I almost told him to knock on the table three times fast and say "No take backs."

Later my cousin Steve came into my bedroom where I was leaning out the window watching Uncle Jim and Aunt Margaret have their usual big whisper fight in the back yard, and he kicked me in the leg as hard as he could. "If your dad breaks that tape recorder, that's it," he said. "I'm killing you." And then he said what he always says to me every time we are ever alone together and probably always will say even when we are both as old and shriveled up as two ancient pieces of gum stuck under a chair. "And if your dad and mom die, and if my dad and mom die, remember you owe all that money to *me*."

◎ Piano Lessons

When I was eight, Aunt Margaret bought Ellen a whole piano in honor of her twelfth birthday and also because Aunt Margaret wanted their lives to be surrounded by the sounds of beautiful music. She said she wanted to give me the same great opportunities Ellen had and that if Mom would just pay for my lessons, I was welcome to practice on their piano. Aunt Margaret told Mom I had begged her and begged her to please let me take the lessons with Ellen and she couldn't bear to see me be underprivileged, but I don't remember ever begging her to let me take any piano lessons. And even if I did, I was only in third grade. Later Mom found out that the actual reason Aunt Margaret wanted me to take piano was so she could get a cut rate for bringing the teacher another kid.

The teacher was this lady whose apartment smelled like a lot of cats. She lived downtown on a street with bums walking on it, and when we would pass one my Aunt Margaret would look at the bum and then look at me and Ellen to make sure we could see how much she was willing to suffer in order for us to learn the piano.

Aunt Margaret would stay until after Ellen's turn, and then they would leave to go wait for me at the Woolworth's lunch counter, and I would be alone with the music lady who naturally scared me because she was always talking loud and sweating big sweats under her arms and yelling "Tempo! TEMPO! goddamn you!" She would grab my hand and pound out the time with it like I was too stupid to count. It was always the same song over and over. "Ten Little Indians." Ellen was already on "Carnival in Venice," and I was still stuck playing "Ten Little Indians"

After my lesson I would walk down First Street three blocks fast, following my aunt's instructions to quit my bad habit of stopping to stare at interesting people. Then I'd turn up Cresswell Avenue, go one block, then go into the Woolworth's, walk through the candy, the makeup, the ladies' nightgowns, then over

13

to the counter where Ellen would slide off her stool and tell me what she just ate.

I was supposed to practice more than I did, but Uncle Jim developed a problem of not being able to stand the sound of the piano when I played it. And then before I knew it, it would be the day to walk past the bums again.

Lucky thing for me something happened to that lady. Who knows what, but we went there one time and knocked and knocked and finally a man in an undershirt opened the door behind us and said "She moved. Do you mind?"

◎ The Tape Recorder

On the Saturday that my aunt and uncle finally left for vacation, my dad borrowed a lot more things than the tape recorder, which meant Lucy and I had to go to our room so that Mom could discuss the fact of that with him, and then finally he called us to come out and we saw the tape recorder set up on two dining room chairs in the middle of the kitchen .

All of us took turns talking into it. Even Mom finally talked into it after my dad played back her voice trying to explain to him why she didn't want him laying a finger on anything of my uncle's. When she heard her own voice coming out from the machine, well, I guess she got just as enchanted as the rest of us.

We each took a turn to do something into the microphone to save for the people of the future. My father told the favorite joke of his about the Polish hit man who got paid to blow up a car and then burned his lips on the tail pipe, and my mother recited her beautiful poem, "To err is human, to forgive, divine."

I read my A-plus book report on the book "What is a Rodent?" and Lucy stood up on a chair and sang "Rice-A-Roni," and I remember leaning on the refrigerator and watching her, thinking how perfectly stupid she sounded, and why in a million years would the people of the future ever want to hear something as dumb as that ?

Well it turns out I didn't have to worry about the people of the future hearing any of it because my uncle erased everything we did that day to tape Eddie Arnold singing "Cattle Call" on the Jimmy Dean Show.

◎ My Singing

There were probably a lot of songs that got sung to me when I was little because people will always sing to babies. Especially ones whose nerve problems you think it's going to help. When you get older, you may never have anyone sing to you personally again, but go all over the world and I bet you can't find one baby that has never been sung to.

Take my cousin Ellen's baby for example. I'm always singing to him. And I'm probably not even going to like him when he grows up.

I don't sing to him because I'm stuck up about my singing talents. It turns out I'm a rotten singer. I've been tested. I know it for a fact.

And I don't sing to him because I have to watch him all of the time and I think he wants to hear a bunch of songs. If it was only songs, then why should I sing? Why not just play the radio for him? But when I am alone with him and I touch him, or especially when I open up one of his midget little hands, all of a sudden I feel something moving inside of me, this natural message for him, and how am I supposed to say it to a baby who can't even talk yet if I don't sing it?

When I was little I used to imagine that I was a great singer, the best singer of all time, and that my singing was a secret power that could make anyone who heard it cry from its beauty. It could make anyone cry, anyone in the world, even Bonna Willis my ex-best friend, who used to chase me down the alley on my way home from school so she could beat my ass, shouting at me in front of everybody, "Run Honky Bitch! Run!"

I imagined my singing could make Bonna cry, only it would make her cry for a different reason. When she saw me on TV leaning over our president who had just been shot in the head and whose last request was to hear me sing in order to perform a miracle on him and bring him back to life, then she would be sorry. Then she would be sorry for ever having been mean to me, for ever having pushed me into the corner of the girl's bathroom and slapping me across the face in front of her stupid idiot new friends, I don't care what the reason was for it. She'd cry so hard she couldn't stand it anymore and she'd climb up onto the roof of the school and jump off and bust her head wide open.

◎ My Mystery

You know that feeling of just standing there staring at boiling water like it's hypnotising you and you can't blink? Well sometimes I'll be babysitting alone in the house and I'll start singing to Ellen's baby and I'll get that.

I'll get the shivers so slow like my body is shrinking down from the inside of my skin and I'm starting to disappear. I don't mean I'm turning invisible. I mean it's like the being me is evaporating up and disappearing until all that's left is this shape thing of a girl in a room singing to a baby on a bed, and the shaking and shining sound that keeps coming out of her, moving up through her chest, her throat, and opening and closing her mouth like a puppet head. It's like the whole world just falls off a cliff except for this sound. This sound that's like the glowing dot hanging there in the middle of the dark after the picture is turned off the TV set.

And if you don't know what I am talking about, I just don't know of any other way of explaining it to you.

◎ Bonna Willis

I was sitting on our porch the first time I saw Bonna Willis going down my street. She was wearing a pink dress and walking with her little brother Elvin, and I wondered if she was my same age because there weren't any girls my age in our neighborhood.

I stood up and shouted "Excuse me girl!" when she was down at the end of the block and turning the corner and she didn't answer me, so I figured either she was hard of hearing or boy was she ever stuck up.

◎ The First Singer

The first actual singer I ever knew was my grandmother, who it turns out wasn't actually a singer. I just thought she was by the way she would move her arms dramatically when she stood up to sing for us about five times during every special occasion party we ever had. My Aunt Margaret used to close her eyes and say "God help us" whenever she saw my grandmother start to get up out of her chair.

She sang songs that weren't even in English, and would make my father and Uncle Jim and my other uncle, Arden, stand up and sing some of those songs too. They always said no no no until she brought up their father who was killed in the war and what would he think of them saying no to her like that when she didn't have many years left on this earth, and then they would all stand up and act like it was the worst moment of their whole lives to have to sing, and the only reason they were doing it was because she was old, she was mad and she was their mother.

But if they hated it so much how come they would always keep going and keep going and end up singing about five million songs nonstop until Aunt Margaret had to finally walk past Uncle Jim while touching her forehead and squinting her eyes and saying to everybody please don't mind her, she just was going out to wait in the car with another splitting headache until Uncle Jim was ready to go home.

And if you think my Aunt Margaret is the Queen of Dirty Looks, you should have seen my grandmother right then.

◎ *The Last Singer*

The first special occasion party we ever had where my dad and uncles didn't sing was the one after my grandmother died. There was no one left to beg them to do it anymore except me and Lucy, and they would say no no no but look sort of interested until Aunt Margaret would keep on changing the subject. So I never heard any of those songs again except for one time when my father started singing a couple from under some bushes he had crawled into during a Labor Day picnic. I remember me and Lucy squatting down and listening to him through the leaves and that was when we heard him go into one of his English numbers, "If she has a freckle on her butt she is nice." A song Lucy never forgot even though he wished out loud about a million times that she would.

I remember I learned some of my grandmother's songs. I can remember her sitting on the couch and me pushing on her knees, rocking them from side to side and singing all those words to her that meant nothing to me except they would make her laugh so hard that my mother would yell from the kitchen, "Enough! are you trying to kill her?!"

And now I can't remember even one of those songs. After a while it's just too hard to remember words that aren't even words to you, you know? It doesn't make sense, does it, how you could do something so perfectly when you were seven that you can't do now.

If back then was now, if my grandmother was still alive and I was sitting beside her again when she was singing, I would for sure take down some notes. I swear to God I would. I learned my lesson. I would write down every one of all those words, I'd sound them out and even if they weren't spelled exactly right it would at least be something, wouldn't it? And for the music, maybe I would draw a kind of a picture of how the song sounded, or maybe just a picture of my grandmother singing. And maybe I would even steal my uncle's tape recorder just to finally catch her voice on it. I asked my mother why she never wrote down any of those songs, and she said where was she supposed to find the time to do that? All she ever did was work, work, work. "Go ask your father why he never wrote them down, if you can find him, the son of a bitch."

◎ The Night

One of the first things Uncle Jim said after he found out Ellen was going to have this baby was " Well you can just thank God your grandmother is already dead because if she wasn't, *this* would kill her. It would! Death is a *blessing* compared to *this*. Can you even *begin* to imagine the pain you would have caused her??! A *mixed* baby! You *ungrateful, filthy, little*—" And then, of all things, he starts to cry.

I know what he said because I was there. I was there sitting at the top of the stairs in the dark with my head against my knees. Ellen had begged me and begged me to please spend the night, the night she had to tell them.

◎ Forgiveness

Ellen's mother said if she had known that Ellen was going to turn out the way she did, she would have strangled her when she was born, and then she points her finger at me and says "Now *you* I could understand; alone in the house, mother always at work, no father—worse!—A bum for a father! But Ellen ? Jesus Christ! Ellen! Why? How? HOW?? Let this be a lesson to you! Don't you ever put you mother through this kind of hell! Don't you ever try to kill your mother this way!" And I stood up just in time to keep her from slapping me.

My mother has told me over and over to please keep in mind that Aunt Margaret was sick with grief the night she said those things, so forgive her for the love of God and forget about it. Mom says she's forgiven her. She said she lit a candle for her at St. Anthony's.

Aunt Margaret wouldn't have anything to do with Ellen after she found out. And do you know she has never once laid eyes on this baby? She doesn't even live ten blocks away. " Couldn't bear it," she says. "It would kill me." Like it's the baby who's the problem.

Can you believe that's who this baby gets stuck with for a grandmother? Is that any fair? From the way things are going, if this was a fairy tale, I know this baby would turn out to be a king.

◎ The Console

In the beginning of our house there was a lot of music playing all the time. My parents kept the console in the kitchen because it had the smoothest dance floor.

We got it second-hand from Uncle Jim, who sold it to us after he got promoted to something big, King of the World, probably, from the way they were acting about it. Aunt Margaret wanted to get rid of everything old they ever had because none of it was going to match everything new they were going to buy. Even after we paid it off, whenever Aunt Margaret came over she would look at it and shake her head like it was still hers.

The console was a big tall thing, too tall for me and Lucy to reach into without standing on a chair, and the lid had a way of suddenly falling WHAM! right onto our fingers to remind us we had no business playing with it, but it was hard not to give our plastic barnyard animals rides on the turntables sometimes.

It was made of a red-colored wood that Lucy eventually scratched her name into with a nut pick, or part of her name anyway, before she got caught, and in my opinion Mom just should have let her finish it. It would be better than having to look at "L U C" for the rest of our lives. Maybe sometime when I'm old enough, I'll buy some wine and me and Lucy can get drunk and put the Y in in the right handwriting.

We all did our best to take good care of the record player, but after all of the knobs were missing and you had to start turning it on with pliers my mom started calling it "that piece of junk".

"Well, at least that piece of junk still works. We can be thankful for that," she says almost every time she puts a record on it and it plays a little slower than it would on another record player, but we are used to that by now.

For me the best part of that record player was the silver and black upholstery cloth stretched tight over the speaker area which I could not resist poking pencils into even though I knew it ruined it. The way the point of the pencil would punch through the fabric and the sound it would make gave me such a strange, perfect feeling in my pants, and listening to music with this feeling was all I ever wanted to do for the rest of my life.

I remember one time just sitting beside it, listening to Elvis Presley's beautiful voice singing about him and me going swimming together in the moonlight. I was listening, listening, listening, just staring at the dust floating in the air, feeling so hypnotized, punching the pencil in and out of the cloth over and over, until I suddenly noticed my mother's legs about five inches from my face.

When I looked up at her she grabbed her forehead and said "Why do you insist on doing that? Is it to torment me? Are you trying to torment me? "

How could I explain to her the feeling I couldn't even explain to myself?

◎ My Record Player

My father came home one day with a present that I thought was going to change my life. It was my own record player that I had to share with Lucy. It was a little boxy thing, the kind that will only play 45s. He said he got it from a guy at work, but later I found out that it had belonged to the kids of a girlfriend we didn't know about yet. The one he would eventually marry and introduce to us one day by rolling down his car window and pointing his cigarette at a woman with a scarf on sitting across the seat from him, saying "That's your, your . . . , whaddaya call it. Your stepmother."

Before he gave the record player to us, he had the idea to spray it with a heavy coat of red enamel paint and he painted every part, including the needle and the masking tape holding the tone arm together. And he must have tried to pick it up when it was still wet because one day, a long time after he was gone, I found it sitting in the basement and I noticed for the first time the print of part of his hand on the side. It made me think of fossils, a million years old.

◎ My Father

If you try to talk about my father to Lucy now, she'll say she doesn't remember nothing about him, but I think she is just being stubborn. I remember everything. Sometimes I remember so much I about hate him for it. Everybody was sad when he left. I think even the dogs in the street were sad.

When he had the days off sometimes we would play a game with him called "Get Lost," where he would take us on long rides all over in any direction and bet us our allowance that we couldn't get him lost. He would turn wherever we said, and when we'd ask him "Are you lost yet?" he'd say "Nope."

I have a song that automatically reminds me of him and sometimes when I hear it by accident I imagine that it secretly means he is thinking of me right then and the song is the sign of it. Sometimes it comes on the radio while we are eating dinner and I feel like I am seeing something in the room that no one else can see. Do you think it's possible that a song could be a message from someone?

And I don't know why that song would remind me of him because we never had the record of it and I never heard him singing it. It wasn't a special song to me at all. It was just a song that probably played on the radio all of the time when things were normal and I never even noticed that they were.

My mother has the same kind of song about him. It's called "Chances Are." Lucy put it on our red record player one day while my mother was in the basement with us folding laundry, and Mom started to sing with it and then all of a sudden she stopped. She put the clothes down, walked up the stairs, went inside her bedroom and closed the door.

◉ The Night Club

In honor of our new record player, Lucy and I created The Record Player Night Club in the dark part of the basement between the door to the garage and the furnace with octopus arms twisting up in every direction. I knew right then that the record player was something very important to us, because normally both my sister and I avoided that furnace whenever possible.

We dragged over an old wooden table across the concrete floor and pulled out a long black extension cord that plugged in by the washer. We hammered nails in all over the walls and along the edges of the wooden table and hung the 152 records our dad gave us on each one. Then we both carried the record player down the stairs one step at a time slowly and carefully like it was a lighted birthday cake.

We picked out a record and put it on. It played. My sister and I just stood there trying to see the title of it while it went around and around. We could not believe how lucky we were.

We acted like we were inspectors from England and walked in and out of the room over and over again, pretending we had never seen anything like it before in our lives. We would point to the records hanging on the nails and go "I say my jolly old chap." We wanted to know exactly what a person would think who was seeing the room for the first time, and we decided they would think it looked incredible.

When Lucy held up a record made of clear red vinyl and looked through it, she said it made the room look even more incredible. Lucy told me it looked so good to her that she wished her eyes would just automatically see everything that way for the rest of her life. She ended up walking around the house looking through it so much that Mom had to take it away from her. Mom said it would ruin her eyes and besides, how was she supposed to concentrate anymore with Lucy always watching her through that red record?

◎ My Genius

The night we made the Record Player Night Club I couldn't sleep
from thinking about more and more ideas for it. We could have
parties. We could open up the door to the garage and have
American Bandstand. We could set up charts for rating the
records. "Is this record a Dream? Or a Dud?" We could spray
paint every part of the whole room pure gold and people would
come in and faint from the amazement of it. And finally I
couldn't help it, I got out of bed and walked on my toes down the
hall, and opened the basement door.

The concrete was freezing cold on my feet and I stood in the
dark a long time waving my hand around before I found the string
to pull on the light. The room was still exactly perfect. I started
picking up records and pretending I was being interviewed on
television about the room; how did I think up the idea for it, was
I in fact a genius, was it hard to drag the table over, how many
records did I have, all that.

I wanted to play a record so bad. I wondered for a long time if
I played it really soft could they even hear it upstairs. And then I
remembered I couldn't remember which way the loudness knob
went and what if it was turned up the wrong way? I picked up
the red record and looked at every wall through it and then I had
the perfect idea.

In the darkroom our dad had set up under the basement steps
there was a red light bulb. I took it and screwed it into a light in
the Record Player Night Club. "Boy," I thought, "is Lucy ever
going to be surprised." Being in the pitch dark Record Player
Night Club when only the red light was on would put us in a
perfect mood to listen to records because music sounds so
completely different in the dark.

◎ She Came Over

In our Night Club we invented this dance where we would put the lighted end of a flashlight in our mouths and just move around in slow motion with our cheeks lit up like we were just sad, lonely ghosts who loved all music except for one certain song that would suddenly make us go wild and strangle people, and we were doing this dance when Bonna Willis first pounded on the door that led in from the garage to the record room. You better believe it made us jump.

There are good things about Bonna Willis and there are bad things about Bonna Willis, and right now I shouldn't be caring about any of them because right now we hate each other's guts and I don't guess that is going to change this June the way it usually does when school is out. Now that we're older you can bet all of that's over. I already know she won't be caught dead talking to no honky bitch this year, and the same goes for her from me only backwards using the word I won't say.

The only reason me and Bonna ever ended up friends in the first place is because when it would finally get hot outside, and everybody in our neighborhood would take their inner tubes and go down to the lake, we were the only ones left stuck on this stupid street. I could never go to the lake because I might drown and Bonna could never go because her little brother did drown. Yeah he drownt. He drownt and that is part of the reason Bonna's mother acts the way she does and another part of the reason Bonna can't ever go no more than two blocks from her house except for . school, to keep an eye on her in case her mother tries to do something funny again like go down Crowley hill in just a shower cap, but even I can't stand to remember that because I like Bonna's mother. I knew her from when before Elvin died and she was still acting OK. Elvin wasn't the only one of them who died you know, because there was another brother named Cleveland who got shot by accident in Washington D.C. where Bonna lived before they had to come out here to just get away from trouble.

They've got a school picture of him up on their wall and I have stared at it many times even though I feel embarrassed at how he's just smiling and not knowing nothing about what is going to happen to him. I know. Me, a girl he never met in a town he never even saw knows exactly the ending and even after the ending. How his whole family moves away afterwards and leaves the place where he used to live, leaves all the sidewalks and the steps and the doors he used to open and shut, and comes all the way out here to my street. I know how his sister is going to hate this place so much that one time she shouts that she hates him too for making them come here, and how her father will cross that living room flying and slap her across the face in front of He Don't Give A Damn Who. And how that picture of Cleveland smiling will just hang there and hang there on the wall in a house on a street in a city he could never have dreamed of even if he dreamed a hundred million dreams.

Sometimes I start thinking what happened to all his things? His pencils, his shirt, his comb, his shoes, his everything,until I just have to close my eyes and think of something else.

And other times I want to memorize at that picture. Know every part of it. You'd think you could run out of things to notice in one picture pretty fast, but you don't. Every time I look at it I can find something new. Like his chipped tooth or the way the one side of his collar is turned under. How he wrote his name in the corner slanted up and underlined. The way you can tell the pen wouldn't work right, how he had to go over each letter until you could read it: Love From Your Loving Son.

The last time I was there—and I couldn't believe I never noticed it before—I saw a tiny chickenpox scar on his cheek in the exact same place Lucy has one.

I remember once in a magazine I saw three pictures of a man who died falling out of hot air balloon. They showed him getting closer and closer to the ground. One. Two. Three.

Doesn't it seem that if you can take a picture of the thing before it happens, you can stop it? You can stop time long enough to a least yell a warning?

I imagine being able to go back into that picture of Cleveland and save him. I imagine being able to go back and whisper "Look out" into his ear.

And after I saved him, well, maybe he would beg me to be his girlfriend.

◎ Our First Day

Back then, the day she first pounded on the door of the Record Player Night Club, all I knew about Bonna was that I had to watch out for her, everybody did. Because she would get after you for no reason, swearing to beat the asses of everyone in our neighborhood on a rotating basis. That was the main topic of her conversation: ass beating. And it wasn't just all talk and no action either. I guess she's just about the best ass beater I have ever met in my life, boys included.

The news got out to her about us having our own record player and when I opened the door Lucy took the flashlight out of her mouth and shined it right into Bonna's face and said "You have the right to remain silent," and I about fell over when I saw it was her standing there with about ten records she wanted to play. That was a long time ago because Elvin was still alive then and she had him with her, and we still had the rule of no Negro kids can come in our house. At first I worried about how was I supposed to explain the rule to Bonna, and then I suddenly realized that we were in the basement and the door came into it from the garage. It would be OK because they could come inside without ever coming inside the real part of the house.

I had never really seen Bonna close up and the first thing I noticed about her was that for earrings she had little pieces of broom straws with the ends burnt, stuck through her ears.

I asked her way later what was the first thing she noticed about me and she said how much I looked like the what-me-worry guy on the Mad magazine, but she wasn't saying it for offense. You can't control the first thing you notice about someone.

Bonna's records had a screaming sound that I had never heard before, but I tried to look like naturally I had heard them all about a million times. There would be a man screaming; and I really mean screaming, and then all of these people would scream back. She said the man's name was James Brown and told me that the song he was singing was called "Say it Loud, I'm Black and

I'm Proud." I had never heard of being proud about being a Negro so I wondered was this a joke song or what? She told me that black panthers were coming to beat the whitey's ass and I didn't know what she was talking about, so I said "I know that. Who doesn't know that?"

She put on another record and told me she was going to do a dance that her cousin showed her called the Tighten Up. "I know that dance," I said.

"Prove it," she said.

I stood there looking at her. "I don't feel like it," I said.

"You lie you die," she said and that made Lucy laugh and say "you lie you die" over and over like it was the best poem she ever heard in her life.

"I'll show you how," Bonna said. "I just learned it from my cousin so I know no one out here knows it yet." She put the needle on the record. "Stand over here," she said, pointing next to her. " Go sideways like this and move your one hand around fast like this and move the other one over like this and when they say the part 'Now make it mellow,' move your arms like this." And she bit on her lips and moved her hands in the shape of tornados.

"I said I just don't feel like it, OK?" and I hoped she would just forget about it.

Bonna said "Watch Elvin do it, come here Elvin, do the Tighten Up, watch him watch him, yeah Elvin come ON! Come ON! He funny, ain't he? Elvin, you think you sly? Look at how he thinks he sly!"

Elvin was only five. I watched him do the mellow part thing perfectly and I felt so completely cheated out of something and I can't even tell you what. Lucy did it too, but she was only Elvin's age so it didn't matter yet how stupid she looked.

Later, after they left and we went upstairs, I told Lucy we had better not tell Mom about Bonna and Elvin, and Lucy nodded her head.

33

◎ My Imagination

That night I imagined me and Bonna becoming best friends.
What that would be like and how everyone in the neighborhood
would start to be afraid of me the same way they were afraid of
her. I imagined naming the Record Player Night Club "Edna and
Bonna's Record Player Night Club At Edna's," and her being so
honored by it she would beat the ass of anyone I said. And I saw
myself being able to do the Tighten Up so perfectly that people
would faint from it. Me and Bonna in the front of the lunchroom
during assembly, doing the Tighten Up for the President's
Council on Fitness. "First Place Award. Now announcing the
winners—Edna Arkins and Bonna Willis." We would put the
trophy in our Night Club. I lay there under the covers thinking
all about it, watching headlights slide across the wall and listening
to Lucy breathing.

◎ Church

For a little while, after Mom got sick and all she could do was stay in her bed with the curtains shut and the lights off, begging God out loud to please make us be quiet, it was Bonna's mother Mrs. Willis who took us to church. But we didn't go to our regular church. We went to a different church that was inside an old store on a street where when we drove down it, our mom would always say "Are your doors locked? Lock your doors so the bogey-man won't get you." It was in the part of town where Mom would point out every police car she saw and tell us to wave.

My sister leaned over to me and whispered "What kind of wacky church is this anyway?" but I tried to sit as normal as possible on a folding chair more beat up than the ones at school, and look like I had been there one thousand times. We sat with Bonna's mother and Elvin, but Bonna sat in the front with some other girls from my school and they were all wearing long gorgeous red robes. A man got up and started to talk and talk and talk, then comes a lady in a beautiful blue tent dress with patterns of golden swirled in it and she had giant arms and her name was Sister I can't remember what. And she sits down at the piano watching the man talk and talk and when he looks at her and smiles she starts to play and begins to sing a song like I had never heard in my life. I couldn't believe perfect singing like that could come out of a real person, a real person who I could go over to and touch with my finger.

She sang with her eyes closed tight, but she was moving her head around like she was watching something and suddenly she made her voice go so low it wasn't even like a lady's anymore and that is when Bonna's mother made me jump by shouting "Go ON! YES!" The more she sang the more people shouted, telling her to go, go, go like it was a race they wanted her to win, and she played faster, and when I looked away from her I saw Bonna in her red robe standing at the front of the room with the other kids, swaying on one foot two times and then the other foot two times and Bonna looked across the room at me and when they started to sing, everyone in the church stood up and started to sing and I looked all around for the hymn book. Where were they getting the song? Where were they getting the words? People were clapping and jumping and I could feel the floor bouncing and the man takes the microphone and shouts into it "YES! COME ON CHURCH! YES! GOD IS MOVING CAN YOU FEEL HIM MOVING!" and I look around and the whole place has gone crazy talking to themselves, pounding their feet, crying, reaching their hands in the air for I don't know what, saying yes lord yes lord and thank you jesus yes my jesus. And that lady is playing the piano so hard I feel the world start to spin, and then Lucy reaches over and starts to yank on my clothes the way she does to Mom when she is scared, and I reach over and pull her arm to stand her up and try get her to act like everybody else so we won't stand out so bad.

I wondered would we get in trouble for this? It was an accident. We didn't know. We thought this was going to be a regular church. You act like this in our church and the priest will send you straight to hell.

After it was over, Lucy and I walked out onto the sidewalk squinting our eyes from the light and stood beside the Willises' car. We saw everybody in front of the church shaking hands, laughing, touching each other on the back and giving kisses, with all the kids running in circles around them like wild Indians, everybody acting like what they all just did in there was the most ordinary thing in the world.

◎ Pimp Walking

The summer I met Bonna none of the teenagers on our block could drive yet and they would all come out onto the street after dinner shouting and chasing each other, doing what my dad called grab-assing, and the rest of us would play three-hour kick ball games in the intersection until it was too dark to see.

And some nights the older boys did a kind of dance parade where they would all get into a line and start singing these things, these poems, about a girl I didn't know named Tracy Chapman, and Bonna told me they were cold blooded poems. The author was Earl Stelly, who would whistle through his fingers and start walking in a way called the Pimp Walk. That was the summer we all wanted to be pimps when we grew up. We didn't really know a lot about pimps except they wore great clothes and jewelry, had nice cars and walked cool, and all of the other boys would jump in line behind Earl Stelly, clapping their hands and slapping their legs and chests, leaning far over stroking their chins and walking the Pimp Walk, chanting "UH! Ahhhh. I Said UH! Ahhh," until they would sound like a train going up and down the block with Earl in front pointing his finger around and singing out his famous poem, "Is Tracy Chapman Like A Cake?" with the boys shouting out the answers. And Earl Stelly must have really loved her, too, because he even had the color of her shoes in that poem. I always wanted to see her, see what was the big deal about Tracy Chapman, but she lived way up on the Crest, on Circle View, somewhere you would never leave to come down over to the street where we lived.

We all thought Earl Stelly was great because he could make up poems about anything. He would do this imitation of a preacher where he would climb up on a car and say "The name is Preacher Deacon Reverend Stelly and I am here to send your asses to fry up in hell." He'd call us Brother and Sister and would sing these preaches, poems about the Bible like "David Messed up Goliath's Head" that he told us he invented, but Bonna told me he was lying because she heard the same poems before on a record. He'd sing the lines one by one, making a noise deep in his throat like he could hardly breathe. One of his poems went

Brother Able was a nigger boy
Brother Cain he was a whitey
Got out into the field one day
Got in a little fighty.
Brother Cain killed Able with a rock
Up jump Able from the dead
takes out his Colt revolver
shoots Cain all full of lead.

He was shouting and rocking the car with his legs until he turned and saw his mother standing on the porch holding a dish rag and watching him and listening to him and did you know it turns out Earl's father who got killed was a real preacher, which all of us only found out right then?

When Mrs. Stelly was done yelling at him, she turned around and went inside and every one of us just stood there until Earl jumped off that car and tore off down Crowley, and if I were him I would have just kept right on going until I reached the other end of the world.

◎ Teenagers

For a while after school, before I was old enough to take care of
Lucy by myself, we'd have to walk all the way up to Aunt
Margaret's and stay there until my mom got home from work.
Both Lucy and I hated that because Aunt Margaret wanted us to
stay in the basement all of the time to keep us from messing up
the plastic she had on her new furniture, and there wasn't
anything to do there except sit around on their old couch in the
part she called their future rec room and read or cut pictures out
of old magazines while listening to Steve practice the trumpet.
After we complained about it so much, Mom finally fixed it with
my aunt to have my cousin Ellen come over and baby sit us for
twenty-five cents for the two hours until Mom got home, which
Ellen said was a gyp because Aunt Margaret just took the money
from her to put toward her college education.

This was a long time ago when Ellen was in junior high school
and still stuck up and mean. A lot of times her best friend Sharon
would come with her and they would sit in our kitchen acting big
and smoking the cigarettes they stole from Sharon's mom, who
must have had a pile of them not to notice. Ellen hated us and I
knew it but I loved her and Sharon because they were both so
beautiful and developed. I didn't even care when they invented a
game of ignoring Lucy and me, saying "Did you hear something?
It must have been the wind," whenever we would try to talk to
them. In a way it was good because if I didn't exist, they couldn't
tell me to go bug off when I sat there on the floor leaning against
the stove watching them and listening to every word they said and
imagining how great it would be to be them.

◎ My Disappointment

When we made the Record Player Night Club all I could think about was wait until Ellen saw it. She would realize I was a genius and she'd start begging me to spend the night with her and go downtown with her and always hang around with her for the rest of her life, amen. I practiced how at first I would say "Nope. No way. Serves you right for ignoring me so much all those times," and then after she begged and begged and begged I'd finally give in and she would be so happy we would wear matching clothes and she would put makeup on me like she did one time before she became such a snob.

I sat on the back steps with Lucy waiting for them to come around the corner and it seems like it took a million years, and when I finally saw them I stood up to unlock the back door with Lucy pushing behind me.

"I get to show them," Lucy says.

"No way Lucy," I say. "I'm showing them." It wouldn't do Lucy any good to show them. She was way too young to hang around with Ellen and me anyway.

"Then I'm coming with. I am," Lucy said. Why did she always have to be so stupid about everything?

"Aren't either, so forget it," I said, and I pushed her and she fell off the steps. I said I was sorry and I tried to tell her I didn't mean to push her that hard but she started crying anyway. Lucy went into our bedroom and slammed the door and I heard Sharon say to Ellen, "What's wrong with the little brat?" and if I wasn't so in love with her I would have kicked her in the leg for calling Lucy that.

It took me a long time to make Ellen and Sharon act like they could hear me and come down into the basement. But when they came down the stairs behind me all I could think of was how they were not going to be able to believe how mod it was.

I told them to stand by the washer and just wait a second.

I pulled on the string and the light came on red. I turned a song on the record player. Then I stood in the middle of the room and yelled "OK!" and watched them walk in.

"Neat!" said Ellen.

"Wicked!" said Sharon.

Ellen picked one of my favorite 45s off of the nail and read Sharon the title. "'Birddog'. By The Everly Brothers. God, I just love that song, don't you, Shar?" and then I saw her turn her head to hide that she was laughing. Sharon picked up a record and said "Ellen, 'Volare!' Your favorite!" And she handed Ellen the record and Ellen said to me "Come on Ed, let me borrow this one. I just have to borrow this, OK? Please?" and then they both started laughing.

That was the day I finally learned that it's not good enough just to have a record player and a bunch of records. You have to have a bunch of the right records. And it doesn't matter if you like the records you have because there are only certain songs that are good to listen to. All the rest are corny. It turned out all the ones that we had were corny.

Ellen asked me if I was going to have a Shindig party here sometime and would I invite her, and I told her to just go shut up and flake off and get out and drop dead and they acted like I had just told them the funniest joke in the world.

◉ It's Not For Me To Say

It was summer right before dinner the first time Mom had to go to the hospital. Dad told Lucy and me as they went out the door to get into our pajamas and sit still without moving on the couch until Aunt Margaret came to get us. He closed the door and Lucy said "Is Mom going to die?"

"No way" I said, but I saw the blood in the bathroom. We waited and waited and Lucy wanted to turn on the TV, but I wouldn't let her because Dad said not to move and I wanted us to be as good as possible so we wouldn't jinx Mom.

Aunt Margaret came into the house and told us to get our shoes and coats on. It felt crazy to be wearing shoes and coats with pajamas I remember, and it was still light outside and I felt embarrassed because some of my friends were still out goofing around and they saw us come down the stairs dressed like that and get into my aunt's station wagon. Nee Nee Davis held up her hand and waved when we went past her, but I didn't wave back and I hoped she would figure out that she had made a mistake, that who she saw wasn't me and wasn't Lucy.

Lucy was stupid enough to ask Aunt Margaret if Mom was going to die. "Good God no! Jesus they got good doctors now! Good ones! They'll take care of your mom, don't you worry at all. You'll make it worse for your mom if you cry, you understand? Fish some kleenex out of my purse, will you Edna? I think there's a stick of Juicy Fruit in there but you'll have to split it," and then she bit her lips and closed her eyes for a second and when she opened them she looked at us with a look I have never seen on her before. She looked—I don't know how else to say it—friendly.

The radio was on and that was the first time I heard that song, the one I hate. Johnny Mathis singing "It's Not For Me to Say." When I hear it all I can think of is that very day riding in the front seat with Lucy leaning against me and the smell of Juicy Fruit gum making me feel like I was going to throw up. How can a song do that? Be like a net that catches a whole entire day, even a day whose guts you hate? You hear it and all of a sudden everything comes hanging back in front of you, all tangled up in that music.

I was worried about Mom but I when I got really scared was when I saw Ellen standing on the front steps in her socks, crying, and then Aunt Margaret yelling at her to get the hell back inside. Ellen wasn't supposed to tell us about what happened to Mom, but it was from her I found out that there had been a tiny baby that I guess just died.

Ellen let me sleep with her in her bed for the week we had to stay there. Sometimes it doesn't matter that your dream finally comes true, does it? She slept with her radio playing and during the night when I couldn't sleep I would lay there and wonder if I had heard every song in the world yet.

◎ Saturday Morning

On Saturday morning when I woke up, Ellen was already out of the bed. I went down the stairs and saw her dancing bent over like a drinking straw to a music show on TV. She had her face about one inch from the screen and her arms stuck straight out to the sides and she was jumping up and down on each foot like an Indian dance, and of course Lucy was right behind her doing the exact same thing. When I walked in I could hear them saying "Go- Go, Go-Go" over and over, and for the first time in my life, Ellen looked completely ugly and stupid to me.

I went into the kitchen and poured some cereal and the phone rang so I walked over to get it and I picked it up and it was my mother.

"Edna," she said. Her voice sounded like I was dreaming. "Edna, are you being good?" And that was the only time I started to cry.

When Lucy heard me say "Mom," she ran into the room and was jumping and shouting and trying to grab the phone out of my hands. She kept sticking her head in my way and screaming "When are you gonna come home?! When are you gonna come home?!"

"Shut UP!" I said. "I can't hear! At least will you please SHUT UP?" and I climbed on a chair to get away, but Lucy kept yelling and screaming and pulling on the phone cord until I just gave up and handed the phone to her.

I went across the kitchen and stood at the back door and pushed my face against the screen until I could finally feel the air from the outside. I stood there a long time not looking at anything and not thinking of anything until I felt a tap on my shoulder, and when I turned around it was Ellen, smiling and handing me a piece of cinnamon toast. Perfectly gorgeous, beautiful Ellen.

44

◉ Mrs. Loximana

The morning after the first night my father didn't come home neither me or Lucy said anything, we just ate our cereal and kissed Mom good-bye like that morning was the most normal morning of our lives. I can remember waking up and seeing Mom at the kitchen table and I knew she had been sitting there all night. Somehow even Lucy knew to do her the favor of keep acting normal.

When Lucy and I got back home from school, Mom wasn't home and there was a note on the door to go to Mrs. Loximana's, the Filipino woman who lived across the alley, whose shiny red bedroom curtains Aunt Margaret always made jokes about. We had seen Mrs. Loximana and her husband before, getting in and out of his blue truck with all of the lawn mowers and rakes sticking out of the back, but we didn't know them.

"Why don't we just go over to Aunt Margaret's?" Lucy asked. But Aunt Margaret would want to know why and I just felt too tired to come up with a good enough lie right then.

We walked across the alley and up the path with terrible feelings. Since I was the oldest, I had to ring the doorbell. Mrs. Loximana opened the door. She was old and about my same size. She was wearing a girl's lime green cardigan sweater embroidered with a big red bird, and a bright pink dress covered with tiny yellow flowers, and she had blue kleenexes hanging out of every pocket. On her bare feet were the weirdest rubber bedroom slippers I had ever seen. Like they had taken every color of ball in the world and melted them together to make her shoes. She was smoking a cigarette, her hair was in a bun and she had a band-aid on her forehead.

"Come in! Come in!" she said, and she moved her hand in front of her face like she was fanning her nose. Lucy couldn't help it and asked her where our mom was, was she going to get our dad, and just from the way she said it I all of a sudden knew that Lucy was about to start crying. "Don't worry!" Mrs. Loximana said, only how she really said it was "Don't wordy!" She leaned down and smiled at Lucy and then suddenly clapped her hands right in front of Lucy's face, which if she would have done to me I would have wanted to slug her, but it made Lucy jump and then made her laugh. "Oooh. See?!" Mrs. Loximana said. "Don't wordy! You still too young!" and you would just have to hear how she said it because it's not normal talking. Every word goes up high at the end like a turkey gobble. It's hard to explain, but if you ever meet any Filipinos just ask them to talk English for you and you will see what I mean.

The first thing she asked us after we came inside was if we were hungry. I had heard not to ever eat at a Filipino's house because they eat dogs so I told her no, but Lucy was too stupid to take the hint and said yes even though I pinched her. Mrs. Loximana pointed us to sit down on the couch that was covered with a bright green bedspread and said "I make you some bola bola! It's gud! It's so gud! My Golly!" and then she bent down to Lucy and sort of jumped toward her with both hands out. I could tell she was Lucy's new hero because I had to grab onto Lucy's sweater as hard as I could to keep her on the couch.

I sat there pretending to watch whatever it was that was on TV and smelling some smells I had never smelled before and sneaking looks all over the place. On the walls were big wooden carvings of people standing around with their arms held out and glasses balanced on their foreheads or bending over and holding long poles with other people jumping over them. She had a cross of Jesus over the top of every doorway and some of the crosses had some dried up leaves and rosaries hanging on them. Also there was a big rug of the Last Supper nailed onto the wall with big nails in each corner and on one of the nails, hanging from a pink ribbon, was a plastic black doll baby like you win at the fair with hoop earrings and a red mouth and eyes that look open or shut depending on where your head is.

I looked across the dining room into the kitchen to see Mrs. Loximana holding the yellow phone between her neck and her shoulder, leaning forward as hard as she could and pulling the cord straight out of the wall like a tightrope. She was standing there reaching her arms out to the front of the stove where loud things were frying. Even I knew that was no way to treat a phone cord. When Mrs. Loximana got off the phone she put down two plates, no silverware, and a big dish of yellow balls of rice on the table and said "Come on now you eat! Eat!"

I told her again I wasn't hungry, but she said to come sit down anyway, and as Lucy was about to put a rice ball in her mouth I whispered "dog meat." "What is de meat?" Mrs. Loximana said. And I wanted to die. "It's bacoln. Bacoln! It's gud! Don't your mommy gib you bacoln?"

"No, that's not what she said," Lucy said. "She said dog meat. You know," and then my sister barked.

Lucy ate about every one of those rice balls. The only thing Lucy thought was crazy about Mrs. Loximana was she didn't have any milk.

It was already dark outside and our mom still wasn't home. We sat with Mrs. Loximana on the couch, watching her watch a contest show on TV where if the contestants got it wrong she'd yell "Estupido!" and I swear to God about this but no one believes me, she was smoking a cigarette with the lighted end in her mouth. When we finally heard the front door open, we were disappointed that it was just Mr. Loximana carrying his lunch pail.

Mrs. Loximana went into the kitchen to make him dinner and I could hear them talking in their language and I knew they were talking about us. And then Mr. Loximana, who could hardly say any English at all, came across the dining room and stood at the boundary of the rug and and waved at us like we were far away, saying "Hello! Hello!" and then did that one trick, you know, where you pretend like your finger is cut off but it's really only your thumb folded over. Then he said "Tank you!" and walked back into the kitchen.

47

◎ The Sound Of Music

"The Hills Are Alive With The Sound Of Music" was the best movie I ever saw and the best music I ever heard. Our whole class went on a field trip to the Blue Mouse Theater to see it and I had to sit up on my knees and keep my balance with my arms so my chair seat wouldn't keep flipping me up and making me miss more of the show.

All I ever wanted to be in life was the star of that show. Someone who sang like a record and ran and twirled around in the mountains, someone so perfect that even nuns could not understand her, someone who said big deal to the Germans and risked her life to save the sad children she was babysitting, and then their rich gorgeous handsome father who thought his whole life was ruined until she came along is now so happy and thankful that he forgets all about feeling bad about his dead wife anymore and then falls madly in love with me. Me, beautiful me with the British accent who can sing so beautifully that everybody immediately knows that I am God's first pick, no contest.

◎ Mrs. Espere

We had a lot of singing in the second and third grade. The truth is my teacher then was a great singer and taught us a lot of exciting songs.

We sang at all the assemblies, and the All City, and creamed the other classes with our numbers. Everybody knew my teacher had the best voice in the whole school. "The colored people do sing pretty," my Aunt Margaret said to my mother in the car on the way home from the Christmas Pageant. "Did you know," Aunt Margaret says to me, "that in my day there were no colored teachers teaching in the schools like there are now? Mrs. Espere is the first colored teacher in this whole school district. She made history, you know." And the way she said it, it was like Mrs. Espere just got away with something big.

The songs Mrs. Espere taught had parts in them to stand up and sing just by yourself. You stood up beside your desk in the middle of a song and it would suddenly be just your voice in the room, you singing a part alone and then the sound of the whole class singing back to you, and the feeling you would get from looking at Mrs. Espere, singing all by yourself, the way she would tilt her head back and smile, like she was holding you up in the air with her eyes, like you were the absolute best thing she had ever seen in her whole life, well, it made you just feel like you could take off flying. For that, even the shyest ones would raise their hands for a turn.

◎ Mrs. Hosey

You think that in the future things can only get better and better, right? I thought that until my fourth grade teacher Mrs. Hosey. Music just wasn't that big to her I guess, because she didn't teach it, she just had us watch it on the educational TV while she walked up and down the aisles whacking our desks with a ruler if we showed poor participation skills.

The TV music teacher was named Miss Gwen, who was always hurling her arm up and down to show us where the note went. She had a skinny helper named Mr. William, whose beard looked like a perfect black tea bag had grabbed right on to his chin. His job was to stand in the background and keep time by clapping his hands without making any sound and making a face with his mouth open, and this look on his face like you were a baby about one year old. There was also a helper named Mr. Pitch, who you never saw. He was just a sound.

Miss Gwen would move her magic hand around and tell us to sing back the line she just sang to us. She would put her hand behind her ear and lean forward like she was actually listening to our voices and before we were even done singing it, she'd nod her head and say "That was excellent!"

I'll tell you one thing, it is hard to get excited about singing back to a television.

◎ Music Appreciation

Well one thing that they never tell you in the grade school is to enjoy singing while you can because eventually you are going to be divided up by who can sing and who can't sing, and the people who can sing will go to Choir, and the ones who can't sing won't sing, and may never sing again, and go to the class called "Music Appreciation" where a teacher will give you a piece of cardboard printed with the life-size keys of a piano and then teach you how to play "Go Tell Aunt Rhody" on it to a record.

How you get tested for your singing is, the first week of junior high school you report to the auditorium during music period and find out you have to stand alone on the stage except for a ninth grader playing the piano, and sing "America the Beautiful" while the rest of the class sits around drawing on their folders or staring at you while they wait for their turns. You get a score and then that's it. The End.

If you are too scared to sing by yourself, you can forfeit, but you automatically go to Music Appreciation. It's a big school and they don't have time to fool around.

◎ Real Music

In the fourth grade Mrs. Hosey said "Hold up your hand who's ever interested in playing an instrument," and I raised my hand because I didn't know she was talking about real instruments. I thought she meant the third grade kind we had in the music box in Mrs. Espere's class. The finger cymbals and rhythm sticks and the triangle. When she told us we had to make appointments to meet Mr. Madsen, the music teacher who came to our school on Thursdays, I realized "Oh. Real music. Real instruments."

Ever since I started school, I had seen people carrying their instruments and I always wanted to carry one. I wanted to carry it to school and I wanted to carry it home. I wanted to yell at people for almost making me drop it in the mud like my cousin Steve yells at me when he carries his trumpet through the alley and I shove him. I wanted to get excused early to go practice in the band, and I wanted to play in every assembly. So when I realized exactly what Mrs. Hosey was saying, even though I was sure my mom would say no, I raised my hand to get an appointment.

On the day of my appointment I left reading to go talk to Mr. Madsen in the lunchroom. I walked in and saw him sitting there at the end of table nine. I had seen him before about a hundred times at assemblies and walking around, but I had never seen him close up or talked to him in person.

The first thing you notice about him is he is short for a man and he really doesn't look very friendly. He has tiny light yellow teeth and his hair is cut so you can see right through to the white skin on his head. And no matter what you are doing, he always looks at you like you are giving him the biggest headache.

I pulled out the chair and sat with good posture and my hands folded. He had a stack of white dittos in front of him. He said "Your name?"

I said "Edna Arkins."

He said "Spell that?" I spelled it.

He said "Instrument?"

I said "Yes."

"No. What instrument? Which instrument?" I just looked at him. I hadn't gotten that far yet. The only instrument I thought I had a chance of getting a hold of was my cousin Steve's trumpet.

"Trumpet," I said.

"Do you have the trumpet?" he asked.

"My cousin Steve does. Steve Arkins. You know him. You teach him."

"A trumpet of your own." Only his fourth question to me and he was already getting mad.

"No," I said. And then, "I'm getting one though."

"The trumpet is a boy's instrument you know. Does your father want you to take the trumpet? Don't you have any brothers?"

"My father's divorced from us," I told him.

"Whose idea was it for you to play the trumpet?"

I almost lied and told him it was my dad's last request. My dad who had been a star on the trumpet but got shot and begged please please that I learn to play it and make hit records every one dedicated to him.

"Me," I said finally. "I had the idea." He looked down at his dittos.

"The trumpet classes are full. Flute. Look up. Flute. You have perfect lips for the flute. Does it matter to your mother what you play? Is she attached to the trumpet?"

"No. Just my cousin Steve is," I said.

He filled out a ditto and handed it to me. "Give this to your mother," he said. "You'll need your instrument by next Thursday, understand? Classes begin on Thursday."

I walked out of the lunchroom, but instead of going straight back to class I walked over to the lavatory, feeling my lips the whole way. I went in and stood in front of the mirror looking at myself, sucking my lips in and out about ten times. Perfect lips for the flute. I didn't want to play the flute, but you can never help what you are born perfect for.

◎ The Flute

I knew Mom would be mad when I handed her the paper and told her I had signed up for flute. She wanted to know where we were supposed to get the money, did I think it grew on trees, did I think she was made of money and then a lot of old son of a bitch stuff about my father, how I should find him and make him buy me the flute, and then on Wednesday she came home late from work with it and put it on my bed.

◎ Mr. Madsen

The flute was a dumb move on my part, mainly because it meant Mr. Madsen in my life. He thought I was disrespectful of music on the very first lesson just because of the STP sticker on my flute case.

Is every music teacher in the world bad? His breath and whole body smelled like old highballs and it about made you sick when he would just take your instrument and play on it like his spit was no big deal, like his spit was God. And he is the most prejudiced person I ever met. He HATED Negroes. He was the meanest to you if you were a Negro. Second meanest: Mexicans and Filipinos. Third: Whatever. Fourth: Tie between Chineses and Whites. Who was he the nicest to? Japaneses. For assemblies it's all Japanese, Chinese and Whites who got picked. You hardly ever saw him pick a Negro, he didn't care how good they were. Even I got picked before they did and I couldn't play anything. No, I couldn't read notes. The only song I could really play great was "The Streets of Laredo," which I learned by just messing around. But it doesn't take any talent to play that way anyway, Mr. Madsen says. "Any idiot on earth can learn to do that. Even a monkey can if you give him enough time."

How the lessons went was, you go in and you line up in order of how good you are except if you are Japanese you go to the front and if you are Negro you go to the end. And right away he is mad at you. "Keep time, KEEP TIME," he says, and he hits your head hard with his wand to the notes like he is only trying to help.

Have you ever met white trash before? The kind that listens to white trash music? The first white trash I ever met was Ranette Bosems who came to our school new in the middle of the year. You could have thought she would be popular at first because she had the longest hair of anyone we had ever seen. Then you noticed the ugly clothes and by third recess you noticed that she was pretty easy to make fun of. It started with her name but it could have started with anything, any part of her. Her last name wasn't really Bosems but that is how our teacher said it at first by accident and when we all started laughing, Ranette said her real name loud and the teacher said "I'm sorry," but it was too late and that is what we called her and if I saw her today that is all I would know to call her because no one remembered her real name after that. Another thing about her was she talked funny and I couldn't figure out what she even was until Bonna called her white trash when she stared at Bonna doing her turns on the monkey bars. Then Ranette said it. She said The Word. She called Bonna a nigger. I remember it felt like the whole recess just stopped like in a science fiction movie where someone presses a button and everyone gets frozen except for two people. I have to say I felt kind of sorry for Ranette right then. She was stupid to have said The Word. I never said The Word, even when I was alone. Bonna popped off that monkey bar and was standing in front of Ranette faster than I could see her move.

"What'd you just call me, girl?" Bonna said. Deborah Small and Gina Davenport went and stood by Bonna, but nobody came to stand by Ranette. We all just watched. "Huh hillbilly white girl? What'd you just say to me? Say it again. Say it again so I can kick your ass," and that's when Mrs. Vidrine came and asked what was going on here. Bonna told her Ranette had called her a nigger and Mrs. Vidrine grabbed Ranette's arm and said "Now you listen to me."

"We don't use those words here you understand? You leave those words back where you came from," she said. "They don't have any place here. I don't want to hear that word come out of your mouth again." And she dragged both Ranette and Bonna to the office because the school rules were, no matter who started it, you both get in trouble.

Nobody would ever stand by Ranette. Ranette's germs, no returns. I felt sorry for her in a way because she couldn't help it if she was a hillbilly. Whenever she walked by, Bonna called her "white trash." "Want to see what some white trash looks like?" she'd say. "Go look in the mirror."

About a week after Ranette first came, our teacher sent her out of the room with a note to go get something and when Ranette left, our teacher said "Class, I have something important I want to talk to you about." And then she told us she didn't like the way we were treating Ranette. "Just because she is different than the rest of you is no reason to be mean to her." Bonna raised her hand and told how Ranette had called her a nigger to her face.

"She just made a mistake, Bonna," our teacher said. "Where she comes from, people still use words like that. She didn't know any better. She didn't know that we don't say those things here. She has a lot of things to learn but she won't be able to do it unless all of us help her and are willing to be friends with her." And then our teacher did something that meant that Ranette would be off limits to us for the rest of her life. She assigned her a special friend of the week. The special friend had to play with Ranette during every recess for one week and sit by her at lunch. First she asked people to volunteer and nobody raised their hands. Then she picked me.

Ranette didn't live all that far from us, just down Crowley behind the lumber yard in those houses my cousin Ellen called the boondocks after a song she knew. There wasn't even a street down there by those houses, just mud roads. When Ranette said would I come over, I was thinking that maybe if I went I would get some extra credit points plus I could tell Bonna all about what the inside of the white trashes houses looked like.

You know how Ranette talks funny? Well her mom and dad I couldn't even understand. Accents was the problem. I felt sorry for them getting stuck talking like that for the rest of their lives. Compared to them, everyone I knew was lucky.

Ranette came from down where it was popular to want slaves. Our teacher told us that the people there are backwards people. I looked around at Ranette's house and thought so these are them. The Backwards People. Her mother was in the kitchen listening to backwards music coming out of the radio. That kind of music could be OK if everybody didn't already know that only stupid people listened to it. That it is prejudiced music and if you got it playing in your house you are stupid and prejudiced too. My cousin Ellen would get embarrassed if she even just accidently hit that radio station when she was moving the dialer around. And here at poor Ranette's house they didn't just have that station on, they had it blasting on, louder than we ever played anything at our house.

Ranette showed me to her mom whose hair was in pin curlers and who I couldn't really understand except she embarrassed me by being so nice and saying something like what a pleasure that I came over and did I want something to eat. Once Ranette was in her house she didn't look so full of germs all of a sudden, and we sat down at their table and ate yellow bread that had the most crumbs of any bread I ever saw and drank milk out of blue metal glasses while Mrs. Bosems combed out Ranette's hair and braided it and laughed whenever I had to ask Ranette what she was saying to me. The part that I didn't get was how come Mrs. Bosems could understand me perfect?

After my week of being her special friend it turns out I ended up being real friends with Ranette and I went to her house a lot, but I made her swear to God not to tell on me for it. I felt bad in a way about making her keep it a secret but there was nothing I could do. Was it supposed to be my fault that they had been stupid enough to want slaves? That they had to go and mess up America for everybody?

Our teacher told us that every Negro in the class had come from slaves and that everybody else was probably related to someone who had owned them. That afternoon we had some big fights on the play field. It was the first time I ever got shoved in the bathroom for no reason.

My father said that they should just get some money together and just send all of the Negroes back to Africa. Everyone agrees it was a mistake to bring them here in the first place and they aren't happy, so why can't we just send them back to where they will be happy. I asked Bonna if she wanted to go back to Africa and she said the only place she wanted to go back to was Washington D.C.

Ranette didn't come to school for a whole week and so finally when no one was looking I walked down to her house to see if she was sick. When I turned the corner I saw their door standing wide open and when I came up the stairs I could see that the whole house was empty except for some cardboard boxes and garbage on the floor. I wondered for a while if they all got kidnapped and then I figured no, that's not what happened.

I walked through all the rooms and then I walked into Ranette's. I could smell the smell of her. On the window sill I saw one of her hair fasteners and I put it in my pocket. I stood for a long time with my forehead on her window, digging my fingernails into her hair fastener and just staring at everything she ever stared at.

On the floor of their kitchen I found a pencil and I wrote my whole name in cursive on the inside of one drawer. And if I ever see Ranette again all I can think of is that I am going to sock her in the stomach.

◎ My Uncle

After Dad left, my Uncle Raymond who was a bachelor and a
sailor moved in with us for a while and used to sleep on the couch
in our front room. He was my mom's little brother and I guess
she was used to pushing him around because that's all she did
when he lived with us. Lucy was his favorite, but I know he liked
me too because he would always bring me things from foreign
lands when he would come to town. He always brought Mom the
same kind of perfume over and over, a special perfume that came
in a glass case with a black cat holding the bottle that Mom said
was no big deal because he could get it cheap at the PX. She
would always ask him why he insisted on throwing his money
away on garbage like that when he should be saving it for
whatever it was he was going to do when he got out of the Navy,
and what he ended up doing when he got out of the Navy was
bringing over a giant green bag full of blue blankets, blue
bedspreads and blue clothes and moving in with us.

Mom yells at me and Lucy for fighting, but our fights are
nothing compared to my mom and my uncle's. She says that all he
lives for is today and he doesn't give a damn about tomorrow and
she yells it over and over from the kitchen while she is cooking
dinner and we are leaning against the bathroom sink watching our
uncle comb his hair.

After he was dressed he would walk into the kitchen to call a
taxi and the smell of his aftershave would get mixed in with the
smell of things frying and Mom would make a face and say "Oh
for the love of God ." He'd look at us, then make a face at mom,
trying to make us laugh while he leaned in the doorway saying
our address into the phone.

There was a record he played all of the time before he went out
called "Pretty Woman," and he would just play it over and over
like he could never ever get enough of that song and the singer's
voice sounded just exactly like my uncle looked. He'd always play
it too loud and Mom would get mad at him for it and for the

second before she yelled, all you would hear would be the needle playing all the scratches and the sound of grease popping and cracking. To me, that song was the sound of something dangerous about to happen to someone incredible, someone like our uncle.

He would try to get Mom to dance with him. She has told us a million times what great dancers everyone in her whole family is, and how our dad was a lousy dancer, until he met her. And there is hardly anytime I've ever seen my mother not want to show off her dancing, but she wouldn't dance with my uncle on nights when all he was going to do was raise hell, so he would dance around her alone, pretending he was singing the song to her and she was a bull he was trying to make run through a cape and then a horn would honk outside and our uncle would grab his jacket and take off. The house always felt extra quiet after he left.

I woke up a lot of times when the taxi brought him back home in the middle of the night, and I'd hear Mom get out of bed to help him walk in. I could hear her lecturing him, saying "See? See? What did I tell you?" and she'd help take off his clothes and cover him with his blue blankets. In the morning I'd go look at him sleeping with his mouth open and his hair all plastered to his forehead and blood on his clothes.

One thing is for sure. He did not like hearing the song "Pretty Woman" at full blast in the morning.

◎ The Camping Trip

In the summer between fifth and sixth grade something crazy happened to Aunt Margaret. She saw a TV special on racial prejudice. From then on for about two weeks until she started taking the hula, my aunt's new hobby was improving the conditions of the life of the underprivileged Negro.

I heard her telling Mom that everyone must do their part to help, or the Negroes in our area were going to get as mad as the ones she saw on TV and burn everything we owned right to the ground. "I've seen the show," she said, "and I know what's coming if we don't find an answer."

My aunt's idea of the perfect solution to this problem was to send ten dollars to The United Negro College Fund and take a Negro child on a camp out. In her opinion, teaching them about the wonders of nature as children would keep them from growing up and joining the Black Panthers and then flipping her car over on Dunbar Avenue. "They are in desperate need of alternatives," she said.

Every August Lucy and I had to go on a camping trip to the mountains for a whole week with Aunt Margaret and Uncle Jim and our cousins in order for them to give us the opportunities we needed to broaden our horizons, and this year Aunt Margaret told me to bring along "my little friend," and who she meant by that was Bonna.

Bonna's mother was back in Washington D.C. staying with her sister, so there was no reason Bonna couldn't come except for the fact that she just did not want to go. At least not at first. Then I asked her what was she going to do all day when I was gone and everyone was at the lake? We still pretended that being stuck with each other was the only reason we were friends, but something had secretly happened and both of us knew it. We were real friends whether we liked it or not.

All that summer I would get up every morning and go to her house, or if she got up first she would come to mine and we

would just walk and walk and walk, spending the whole day
doing anything. She was all I thought about. Every day and every
night I would say it in my head, "My best friend Bonna."

When it would start to get dark I would walk her to her house
and then we would turn around and she would walk me to mine
and then we would turn around and do it over and over again
until one of our parents would finally make us knock it off and
come inside. I remember her standing on the front porch waving
good-bye to me and how I walked backwards all the way up the
dark street so both of us could keep on waving to each other until
the very last possible second. And I thought it was going to be
like that forever. I thought that we would get married to twins
and live next door to each other for the rest of our lives.

Aunt Margaret could not believe that Bonna's father wanted to
meet her and Uncle Jim first before he would let Bonna come
with us. "Is that really necessary?" she asked me. "Just what kind
of people does he think we are?"

Bonna got to stay over the night before the camping trip and
we woke up from the phone ringing, my aunt calling to make
sure we would be up on time. It was still dark out when my
mother came into our room and said girls, girls, time to get up.

Me, Bonna and Lucy sat on the front porch leaning on all of our
things, waiting for Aunt Margaret and Uncle Jim to pick us up.
Bonna kept zipping and unzipping her new yellow windbreaker.
The sun was just starting to come over the garage across the street
and my mother came out barefoot in her bathrobe, drinking
coffee, breathing in, and telling us how good the air smelled to
her. She sat next to me on the step and smoothed out my hair a
little with her fingers and smiled at me. Finally after a thousand
years, my aunt and uncle's car came around the corner.

We all let Bonna have the window seat the whole way and
when we got to the campground we drove slowly through the
loops about six times listening to Uncle Jim and Aunt Margaret
argue about which was the best site and finally they picked one

and we got to work unloading. After we set up the tents and the table, Steve took off exploring with his friend Neil, and Ellen took off with Sharon to look for cute guys, and Lucy and Bonna and me crawled around in circles inside of our tent playing name it and claim it for where we were going to put our sleeping bags. Uncle Jim was sitting on his folding chair saying over and over what he said every year. "Seven kids. Seven kids. Jesus H. Christ, Margaret, what do you think I am made of?" only up until this year he always said "six." I was thankful Bonna wasn't white because if she was, it would have been just me stuck with Lucy again, same as always.

After dinner Bonna and me walked past about five campsites to the pump to get water for the dishes. The sun had gone down and people around us had lit their fires and were sitting at their tables playing cards and talking like they were still all in their living rooms but just didn't notice someone had lifted the houses away. The trees started getting that giant look.

"Why does your aunt keep saying to me do I like everything?" Bonna asked me. "Do I like like the mountains, do I like the fresh air, do I like the food, do I like eating off a paper plate. Don't she think I never been outside before?"

"My aunt is a dirty son of a bitch," I said, and we both kept walking like neither of us was scared by what I had just said. I don't know how I said it. I had never said anything like that before in my life.

After we filled the bucket we walked slow and in step to keep the water from spilling onto our legs. "Your aunt ain't so bad," Bonna said, trying to help me take it back.

When we got back to the campsite I saw Aunt Margaret was smiling and waving the dreaded books in the air.—"357 Songs We Love to Sing."

"I found them, honey! Jim! Kids! Sing-a-Long! Sing-a-long time!" Bonna looked at me. I have to admit that was the one part about camping with Aunt Margaret I just sort of didn't tell Bonna about.

We sang the usual numbers—"Polly Wolly Doodle," "Old Dan Tucker," and the one Uncle Jim loved called "My Last Cigar." And then Aunt Margaret saw the writing under the song "Old Black Joe" and decided to give us a history lesson.

"Listen to this, everybody!" But she was looking straight at Bonna. "Stephen Collins Foster, a truly American writer of what are called the folk songs of America, was born July 4th in 1826!"

"Can you believe it?" Aunt Margaret said. "The same birthday as America's birthday!"

"And my dad's," Lucy said, which gave my Aunt a pinched face for a second because as a rule she would rather we didn't mention him because by then she knew she might as well just kiss all that money he owed them good-bye.

"It says here that he wrote 'Oh Susannah,' 'My Old Kentucky Home,' and 'Massa's In De Cold Cold Ground'!"

"Oh for crying out loud, Margaret," my Uncle Jim said and pulled out his cigarettes. "Jesus. Do we really need to hear this?"

My aunt kept reading. "From an early age he was interested in music and he often attended Negro camp meetings and there studied the music of the colored people!"

"Oh!" Aunt Margaret said like she had just discovered the cure for cancer. "So that's how so many wonderful songs could come out of just one little man. He had some very important helpers, didn't he?"

Right before we got ready to go to bed, Aunt Margaret asked Bonna how she was enjoying her very first camping trip. When Bonna told Aunt Margaret it wasn't her first camping trip, that in fact she had been camping about a million times with her cousins in South Carolina, my aunt looked so disappointed I thought she was going to cry.

◎ The Projects

Bonna's mother took off one time while Bonna was over playing with me in my yard, so she couldn't stop her from walking down Crowley, crossing Clanton Avenue, and heading south along Dunbar in her flowered robe and pink slippers and screaming all the way.

A car pulled up into our alley and we could hear a man calling Bonna's name through the laurel bushes and she got a scared expression and said, "My daddy!"

She ran and opened the gate, jumped the dirt step and was gone. I shoved myself into the hedge and listened to her father talking to her. "What you mean leaving your mama like that? Get in here. Do you know she walked all the way to your Aunt Martha's? Now whose fault is that?" He says aunt like "ont." I hear Bonna ask if I can come and I don't hear no answer and I pray to God he is looking at her the way my mother looks at me when I ask a stupid question, that have-you-just-gone-crazy look, but around the corner comes Bonna, balancing one foot on the dirt step and the other in the air like she doesn't even have enough time to set it down, saying "Come on hurry up," and I walk toward her feeling like I am walking out of a store stealing something in plain sight, praying someone will catch me before I get out the door because I know that what I am about to do will get me into more trouble than I have ever been in my life. I am about to ride with a Negro man in his car.

My mom likes Bonna, especially if she is playing at our house. The "no coloreds in the house" rule had to get changed after a while because after the first kids moved out, the only kids that moved in were mostly Negro, Filipino or white trash. "Our street has officially gone to Hell," my mother said when the last two pure perfect white families moved out the same week. "I don't know why I bother working on the yard anymore."

If we had kept the original house rule, then me and Lucy would have to play over at their houses, which my mother felt was a lot worse. She never said this but I figured it out for myself,

66

something she was always asking me to do anyway. I asked her one time why I was never supposed to go to Bonna's house when her father was home, was it because he was a Negro, and my mother slapped my face and told me I knew better than to ask such a question. That everyone is equal in the eyes of God and nobody is better than anyone else but she had her reasons and someday I would understand them.

If she saw me climbing into the car with him and Bonna I'd get the belt and I would deserve it. I duck down low and spread out flat on my stomach across the back seat and pray Bonna won't turn around and ask me why I'm laying down on the seat like that and I feel the car begin to move and I know I can't turn back now. I'm dead. I lean over and feel the car going over some bumps in the alley and then everything smooths out and I can tell from the turns that right about now we are driving past my mother who is bending over the dirt and yanking out the weeds.

I look at the stuff they have on the floor of their car. A green rubber band, a pink curler, some dirt, a church newspaper.

Bonna is in the front seat with her window rolled down and I turn over onto my back trying to tell from the telephone poles if we are out of the neighborhood and I can sit up yet. The air blowing in is hot. I feel the streets I know moving away underneath the tires and I stare up at the roof of the car, counting the places the cloth is torn, brown stuffing hanging out. All of a sudden I see the tall sign for the Wig Wam store float past the window and I know it is safe to sit up.

Mr. Willis isn't saying anything and Bonna isn't saying anything either, just like all we are doing is going to the store to get some baloney and not going down to pick up Bonna's crazy mother. In fact, Bonna is sitting up perfectly straight with her elbow leaning up and sticking out of the window like she's a princess in the May parade about to wave at a crowd.

Bonna's Aunt Martha lives in the Dunbar Vista Projects, the ones with all the laundry hanging everywhere and the kids standing around in the dinky brown yards giving the finger to every car that goes by. "At least we don't live there yet," my father used to say whenever we would drive by, and we would all laugh. If my father was still living with us and it was his day off, he would be taking us to the park or over way across the bridge to Lake Marie, the greatest lake in the world. A lot better than Lake Osage. Lake Marie has big gates you go through, and a man in a booth who waves, and a sandy smooth bottom, and there is no one chasing after you yelling "hey you" and trying to get your money. If my dad were still living with us, I would be in that front seat and it would be Bonna here in the back on her way to a place she had never been before, Lake Marie, a place where I have never seen a Negro, not once, and because of me she would be the first and I would feel proud to show her off.

I had never been inside the projects before. I can't even imagine what it's like to live there in the little mustard-colored houses with flat roofs, flat everything, every house looking exactly like the one next to it.

Mr. Willis drove his car down the slow curvy roads and pretty soon I couldn't see nothing but all these project houses all around with people sitting out on their one front step, staring at who I was in the back of this Negro man's car. I couldn't see Dunbar, the road back to my house, and I felt scared but I kept acting completely normal.

Mr. Willis stopped the car, and the screen door to one of the projects opened and Bonna's Aunt Martha's arm came out with a cigarette in the hand moving in a hurry-up-and-get-in-here motion, and before the door slammed shut I recognized through the screen that Aunt Martha was the lady in the blue and gold tent dress, the singer lady from church. I couldn't believe that a singer like that was smoking cigarettes and living in the projects. Didn't her singing make her almost a queen?

Mr. Willis turns to Bonna and says "Now you wait right here until I get back with your mama. Don't you go nowhere but this front yard, do you understand?" and we sit in the car watching

Mr. Willis go up the step, through the screen door and into the dark house.

We immediately hear Bonna's mother start yelling. "Who the fuck called you, you black assed motherfucker," and Bonna turns and puts her chin on the back of the car seat and says "Let's go for a walk."

We walked for nine or ten houses. I was counting them carefully to make sure that we could get back. We turned left at the project with the piece of rug in the yard and turned right at the one with the silver tape on the window and then kept turning and walking until I couldn't keep track any more and we were lost. I told Bonna that and she just kept right on walking.

"I ain't going back there," she said. "You go 'head but I ain't going back." I don't know if you have ever been somewhere with a friend who you can all of a sudden tell really does not care what you do with yourself, if you stay or follow or whatever. The kind that don't need you to get to where they are going but it turns out you need them. We kept on walking.

Bonna started cutting across yards and going and turning and I knew that now there was no way I was ever going to get back. What were we going to do if any of the rough kids who lived around there started chasing us? I don't know if you have ever been with a friend who called you a pussy for even asking a question like that.

We saw a big building. It looked exactly like all the little project houses only it was twenty times bigger. Bonna said it was the Meeting Hall and she knew they had some pop machines and washing machines down there and I asked her, trying to sound as normal as possible, if they also had an office there with a lady in it and I imagined how nice it would be if the lady in there was Mrs. Boleman, the secretary from our school. How she would look at me and say "Why Edna Arkins! What on earth are you doing here! Let me give you a ride home and drop you off at the bottom of Crowley so that you can walk the rest of the way and your mom will never know you left!" And even if it was just an ordinary lady there and not Mrs. Boleman, I would ask could I use the phone and I would call my mother and tell her I was the stupidest most ungrateful person in the world and would she please come and get me so that she could give me the punishment I deserved and I imagined how I would make myself cry when I said it and how pitiful my voice would sound and how she would feel sorry for me, and I must have started practicing it in real life because Bonna said "What you mumbling about?" and I didn't know I had been mumbling at all.

We started walking down across the brown grass and I had my eyes peeled for a door that said Office when all of a sudden a boy's voice yelled out "UNKA TOM!" and from the way Bonna turned around I knew she knew the yell was for her and I suddenly felt my rear end get ice cold. "Where he at?" she said. I started looking really hard down at the toe of my tennis shoe and then at the grass all around the toe of my shoe. I was just concentrating on that, just like if I kept staring and staring without blinking, all of a sudden I would look up and I would be home.

Bonna yelled out "Where you at, nigger?"

The voice came again. "UNKA TOM UNKA TOM!" It came from the project behind us. Bonna saw the curtain move and she tore up to the window and slammed her hand right into the screen, screaming "Come out here motherfucker so that I can kick your ass calling me Unka Tom. Who's unka tom?! Come on out here."

I say "Let's go back to your Aunt Martha's, Bonna, your dad is waiting. You're going to get it."

"I got to kick this little motherfucker's ass first," she says. Then we hear some little shrimp crying and the screen door opens and this five-year-old walks out wiping his eyes on the back of his hands, and we hear the Unka Tom voice calling him back in the house, calling "Andy! Andy, get back in here, man," and Andy is crying and squinting his eyes up and telling Bonna to go find his mama.

"I don't know where your mama at, boy," Bonna says. Then she walks up onto the porch and calls through the door, "You going to come out here or am I going to have to come inside to kick your ass?" All of a sudden I know this is probably the last summer I will ever spend with Bonna. I have never seen her be so bold. Not even at school where she is the boldest. There's no sound coming from the inside and then I couldn't believe it, Bonna just opens the door and walks right in. Me and the little boy just look at each other. We hear the Unka Tom voice yelling "Get out! Get out or I'm calling the police on you! You can't just be walking into people's houses!"

I watch Andy rubbing one eye with his wrist and then I feel him lean against me. I all of a sudden can feel that I am getting a sunburn. I wonder what I will do if I have to go in there and help Bonna kick that boy's ass. I'm no good at ass kicking at all. I'm not even good at tetherball.

I can hear her talking in there and I can hear him talking and they aren't yelling any more and I watch Andy walk away from me and go inside. I stand there wondering now what until I hear Bonna call my name, and when I go up and look through the screen I can see her and him standing by the kitchen sink smoking cigarettes.

"Come in here," Bonna says. She looks at the boy and says "This why you calling me Unka Tom?" and they both crack up laughing.

I look around. All the window shades are pulled down and it is cool and yellowish inside. The TV is on and Andy is laying on the linoleum watching a margarine commercial. I notice the linoleum they had is exactly like the linoleum at my cousin Ellen's and that makes me feel better. The chairs at the kitchen table don't match and there are pictures of people taped everywhere on the walls, also, the most pictures of Jesus I have ever seen in one place. I want to ask him does your mother collect Jesus but I figure he would slap me silly. To some people "your mother" is a swear word. I stay standing by the door.

"I ain't no Unka Tom" Bonna finally says.

"Then what you got her with you for? I know she ain't your sister," and they crack up laughing again.

I looked at Bonna. Then I looked down at the floor. I was in a Negro project. I imagined what my mother would do if a voice suddenly started talking from out of nowhere like in a laundry detergent commercial and said "Mrs. Arkins, right at this very second while you are trying to untangle that garden hose, your daughter Edna is standing over with some Negroes over inside a Negro project." And I couldn't help it I started laughing.

"That your little brother?" Bonna asked the boy.

"Yeah."

"He cute. Can he swim?" The boy shrugged his shoulders. "If he can't swim," Bonna said, "then you better not let him go to the lake. Does he tell on you for taking your mama's cigarettes?"

"No."

"Can I have the pack of them then?"

"You high."

"Can I take one to take with me then?"

The boy handed her one. He was smaller than her and smaller than me. He wasn't wearing a shirt, just some pants, and I looked at how his nipples—if that's still the name of them on a boy—were even darker than his skin. He had something wrong with his eye. I was trying to see what it was and he caught me and said "What you lookin' at ?"

"Nothing." I said and acted like I was just noticing the wall by his head. Built into the wall was a little fan that was spinning a hundred miles an hour.

72

Bonna said "What is wrong with your eye?"

He said "I was born with it."

It looked like a pink skin like from the inside of his mouth was covering his eye. I wondered if I could ever get used to looking at it. Or what it would be like if he turned out to be my boyfriend, how would I explain it to people.

Bonna pushed away from the counter and said "We got to go. What should I do with this?" She held up the end of her cigarette.

"Put it in the toilet," the boy said.

Bonna handed it to me. "You," she said. I had smoked a hundred cigarettes so I took it and held it professionally and smoked on it once and said "Take a puff. . . . It's Springtime!" and they both started to laugh and I laughed too and I could see the toilet down the hall and I went and threw it in.

While we were walking back Bonna seemed to be feeling better. I know I felt better, and I tried to make her laugh by saying the slogan of every cigarette I could think of. We could be out of here soon. We would get in the car and drive and we would be home. My mother could whip me a hundred whips and it wouldn't even matter anymore, I would still be happy to see her.

When we got to Aunt Martha's the car was gone.

It took us a long time to walk Dunbar. Boys honked their horns and yelled words at us from cars. We crossed Clanton running and finally climbed Crowley, passing the dirt road leading to the boondocks, and came to Bonna's cut-off at the alley.

"You going to get killed?" I asked her.

"If my mama is not acting crazy I will. But if she is real crazy Aunt Martha will be there to calm her down and don't nobody hit me with Aunt Martha standing there." I thought of Aunt Martha with her eyes closed pounding on the piano and singing. I imagined her singing to Bonna's mom and putting cold washcloths on her head. "If she real crazy," Bonna said, "they might not even remember me until next week."

I said see ya and she said see ya and she went up her alley and I snuck around the corner to see my mom still bending over her plants like only one second had passed for her the whole entire afternoon.

◎ Girl Scouts

You know that one song "Kum-bi-ya My Lord Kum-bi-ya"? The most popular song of all Girl Scouts? Well our troop did it every time we got together including all the hand movements, and I'm telling you that was the first song I ever got sick of in my whole life.

They had had a sign-up sheet for who wants to join Girl Scouts at the school and I wanted to get in because I wanted to wear a uniform to school and also because Joycie Myers's mother was the leader and Joycie Myers was the world's most popular girl. If I joined I would get to go to her house all of the time, a house that had been off limits to me because of the fact that she hated my guts. I wasn't the only one though, she hated nearly everybody and it makes you wonder how anybody could be so popular when she hates everybody who likes her?

Turns out I wasn't the only one with the brilliant idea of joining because of Joycie and so many girls signed up that they had to split into two troops divided by which side of Dunbar you lived on. And when they made the announcement at the first big meeting, all the girls who lived on Joycie's side started screaming and the girls who lived on my side got introduced to our troop leader, Mrs. Doucette, who had greasy two-color hair, the bottom part blonde, and was probably the fattest lady I ever saw sing "Kum bi ya." I didn't want to be in Girl Scouts if I had to have her for a troop leader, but I was stuck because my mom had already bought the uniform.

My troop was crossed with some girls from Stintson grade school from across the hill, who probably got divided off from a decent troop the exact same way we did. All I know is that we hated all the girls from Stintson and they all hated us. We couldn't meet at Mrs. Doucette's house, so we would have to rotate meeting at our school lunchroom, and at the Stintson school lunchroom and when we had to go to Stintson we would spit on the playground all the way up to the door and then we would all sit at different tables making remarks to each other until Mrs.

Doucette would come in, always fifteen minutes late and smoking a cigarette. Mrs. Doucette smoked so much that I bet if you did an x-ray on her lungs all you would see hanging there would be two old black bananas.

She had a daughter who was in our troop too and was so skinny that Bonna said Mrs. Doucette snatches the food off of her plate before Theresa Doucette can even get it to her mouth. We invented a game based on Mrs. Doucette called "Mrs. Doucette," where when you weren't watching someone could grab your food from you.

Well after a few meetings of all we did was practically just sing "Kum-bi-ya" over and over as led by Theresa while Mrs. Doucette sat in the back of the lunchroom flipping through magazines, some of the girls dropped out.I wanted to drop out so bad, but my mother would have slayed me for how much the uniform cost so I stayed in and by the fourth meeting there were only twelve of us left in the troop and only three from my school—me, Bonna and a girl named Cora Thomas who didn't mean nothing to either of us back then, except it was her mother who always gave us rides. Now it's Cora and me who are best friends even though I don't like her all that much, not as much as me and Bonna used to like each other a million years ago in the sixth grade which was the last possible time we still could.

"Now in Girl Scouting there is no such thing as the color of your skin," Mrs. Doucette explained when it got noticed that the only people in our troop invited to go to Joycie Myers's all troop slumber party were me, Cora and Theresa Doucette. Mrs. Doucette said Mrs. Myers told her that we were all the extra girls she had room for and that she had left it up to Joycie to choose who she thought would get along best with everyone. I wanted so bad to believe that that was the real true reason, but I had met Mrs. Myers and I knew she was the one who picked Dunbar Avenue as the dividing line for the troops. I knew it and Bonna knew it too and we both knew why.

I knew prejudiced people. Mr. Madsen the music teacher or especially my Aunt Margaret, for example. But Mrs. Myers was different. She never ever said one word you could prove it by, but you knew it right away. She arranged things.

It was the biggest honor of my life to be invited to Joycie Myers's to spend the night and I could not turn it down. She lived on Circle View, she had a canopy bed, she was my dream. And even if Bonna said I was prejudiced for going, I know I wasn't. It's a built fact that there is just no way you can be prejudiced and a Girl Scout at the same time.

One of the girls who wasn't invited told her mother about it and her mother called the other mothers and there were meetings and meetings and meetings and you wouldn't think something like that could ever turn into such a big honking deal but it did. And when it was over, Mrs. Myers said she did more for the community than anyone and look at the thanks she got, quit her troop and took Joycie out of Girl Scouts for once and for all. Most of the girls in Joycie's troop sided with her and quit too, so there was just one troop for our school with girls from both sides of Dunbar, and Lucy is in that troop now. Troop 64.

For me to wear my uniform to school after that was hard. I was still a Girl Scout, so Joycie Myers and all them hated my guts for what we did to Mrs. Myers, but I was a Girl Scout who had gone to the slumber party. It was something the troop would never forget about me until finally sixth grade ended and it didn't matter what anyone thought about anything because the whole world was turning sideways anyhow.

So that is how Cora Thomas and me ended up friends. She had gone to the slumber party too so it was sort of like we both had the same disease. If it wasn't for Cora, I don't know who I would have eaten lunch with because there was just no table for me anymore.

◎ Seventh Grade

From the first day of seventh grade everyone was new. Even if you had known them all of your whole life they were still new. And from the second we walked through the doors we all automatically split apart into groups of who was alike. Everyone knew exactly what to do, like someone was whispering instructions to our hands and eyes and feet and hair. Every kid from my old school, all of us who had ever lived on the same street together and played together all our lives stopped talking and walking with each other and never talked or walked with each other again.

This was our new main rule of life even though it wasn't us who created it. It just grew there, like big permanent teeth after baby teeth.

We had to constantly read books and poems about equality in English, and I wondered sometimes if Bonna ever thought of me the way I thought of her when I read them. *To Kill a Mocking Bird. A Raisin in The Sun*: "What happens to a dream deferred?"

If she didn't that's OK. It wouldn't hurt my feelings.

And we had to write our own stories and poems and discuss them and they would put us in a mood that felt so real and true to us because we could each write the answer and the answer was always the same: love each other, love each other, love each other. And we would really believe things could change until the bell would ring and we would go back out into the hallway and know there was no way some puny poem or story could ever touch this huge big thing. This Kal-Tiki The Immortal Monster.

There were a lot of fights. You would get pushed in the back on your way to class or pushed at your locker. One day I got shoved so bad I cracked my head against a toilet stall and when I turned around I saw who did it was a girl I didn't know standing with two other girls, and one of them was Bonna. For a second I forgot the rule of Bonna and me not talking anymore and I said "Why didn't you tell her? What'd you let her do it for, stupid?" And we both froze. Bonna didn't have a choice. By the time I tried to run it was too late. She pushed me into the corner and her friends stood there watching and I remember looking at her and not believing she would really hit me because I had been to her house, because I knew her mother, because inside we were still friends, we were, I knew it, and I knew she knew it, rules or no rules. When she raised up her hand and slapped my face hard I told her so, I said "Remember? Don't you even remember?" and I started crying, I couldn't help it, and she slapped me again and kept slapping me until I started naming everything in her house— the lamps, the chairs, the TV, the color of the walls, the couch, the rug, and I couldn't shut up and I couldn't shut up and the next thing I knew a teacher was yanking both of us by the arms and dragging us down the hall to the office just like I had seen girls being dragged every day since I got there.

We sat on two chairs in front of the secretary, waiting for the vice principal to come. I turned to look at Bonna and she was staring straight ahead and I could see the streaks on her face.

In the vice principal's office we acted like we had never met. Like all it was was any black girl slapping any white girl who had mouthed off to her, something that happened every single day and would just keep on happening world without end.

When he called my mother to tell her, she never knew the girl was Bonna, just like Bonna's father never knew the other girl was me.

MUSIC NOTEBOOK

Gertrude "Ma" Rainey
1886 – 1939

GERTRUDE RAINEY WAS BORN IN COLUMBUS, GEORGIA TO PARENTS PERFORMING IN TRAVELING MINSTRAL SHOWS. SHE BEGAN HER STAGE CAREER AT THE AGE OF TWELVE. SHE HAD LOW, WIDE HIPS, BIG GOLD RIMMED TEETH, INFECTIOUS HUMOR AND A LEGENDARY APPETITE FOR HARD WORK, YOUNG MEN, AND WILD LIVING. SHE WAS ONE OF THE FIRST PERFORMERS TO BRING THE BACK COUNTRY SOUND OF THE BLUES ONTO THE STAGE AND THE RESPONSE TO THIS WAS OVERWHELMING. SHE WAS ALSO ONE OF THE FIRST BLACK SINGERS WHOSE RECORDS WERE AVAILABLE THROUGH MAIL ORDER AND HER VOICE QUICKLY SOAKED INTO EVERY CORNER OF THE SOUTH. SHE TRAVELED WITH HER OWN SHOW ON THE T.O.B.A. VAUDEVILLE CIRCUIT. (THEATER OWNERS BOOKING ASSOCIATION, ALSO CALLED TOUGH ON BLACK ASSES by THE PERFORMERS.) PEOPLE TRAVELED FAR OVER COUNTRY DIRT ROADS TO SEE HER STEP ONTO THE STAGE FROM THE HORN OF A GIANT VICTOROLA IN A SHIMMERING GOWN, HER WILD HAIR STICKING UP AROUND A GLITTERING TIARA, LONG EARRINGS FLASHING, HER NECK COVERED WITH TWENTY DOLLAR GOLD PIECES, AND SHE'D WAVE A HUGE FEATHER FAN AND MOAN OUT A SONG THAT MADE PEOPLE'S BLOOD STOP COLD. SHE PERFORMED IN TRAVELING SHOWS FOR 29 YEARS. IN 1933, THE COMBINED EFFECTS OF THE DEPRESSION AND THE SUDDEN DEATHS OF HER MOTHER AND SISTER CAUSED HER TO RETURN TO COLUMBUS WHERE SHE LIVED WITH HER BROTHER AND BECAME VERY ACTIVE IN THE FRIENDSHIP BAPTIST CHURCH. SHE DIED OF A HEART ATTACK ON DECEMBER 22, 1939 AND IS BURIED WITH HER FAMILY IN THE PORTERDALE CEMETARY IN COLUMBUS, GEORGIA.

Jimmie Rodgers
1897 – 1933

JIMMIE RODGERS WAS BORN IN MERIDIAN, MISSISSIPPI. HIS MOTHER DIED WHEN HE WAS FIVE AND HE HAD A HARD BUT INTERESTING CHILDHOOD FOLLOWING HIS FATHER, A RAILROAD FOREMAN, THROUGH DIFFERENT CITIES IN THE SOUTH, LIVING ON THE ROAD OR BETWEEN RELATIVES. MANY OF THE RAIL WORKERS WERE BLACK AND JIMMIE SERVED AS THEIR WATER BOY AND LEARNED THE MUSIC THEY SANG. AT 13 HE JOINED A MEDICINE SHOW AND TRAVELED AROUND ONLY TO RETURN TO WORK THE RAILS HIMSELF. IN 1927 HE PUT TOGETHER TWO STYLES OF MUSIC THAT WOULD FATHER COUNTRY WESTERN MUSIC AS WE KNOW IT TODAY: BLUES AND YODELING. HE BECAME A BIG SUCCESS WITH HIS MOURNFUL SONGS ABOUT HARD TIMES, TRAINS AND LOST LOVE, AND BEGAN TO TOUR ALL OVER. HE WAS STRICKEN WITH TUBERCULOSIS BUT COULD NOT BEAR TO REST LONG ENOUGH TO RECOVER. HIS HEALTH BECAME INCREASINGLY FRAIL AND AGAINST DOCTOR'S ORDERS HE TRAVELED TO NEW YORK TO A RECORDING SESSION. HE WAS SO WEAK HE HAD TO LAY ON A COT BETWEEN SESSIONS. HE DIED A COUPLE OF DAYS LATER IN A ROOM AT THE TAFT HOTEL.

Gospel Style

WITHOUT A DOUBT, THE STRONGEST INFLUENCE IN ALL BLACK MUSIC IS THE CHURCH. THE GOSPEL SOUND HAS IT'S ROOTS IN SLAVERY DAYS COMING OUT OF WORK CHANTS AND FIELD HOLLERS AND THE ONLY MUSIC ALLOWED MOST SLAVES: THEIR OWN VERSIONS OF ENGLISH HYMNS. IN THE BAPTIST CHURCHES, FROM CLAPBOARD CHAPLES TO STOREFRONT MEETING HALLS WHEN PEOPLE SHOUTED OUT AND MOANED IN SONG UP TO THE LORD, BLACK CULTURE WAS RE CREATED AND PRESERVED. IN GOSPEL SINGING EMOTION IS ALWAYS RIGHT UP FRONT, OPENING A PLACE IN THE SINGERS AND LISTENERS FOR THE SPIRIT TO ENTER AND TAKE OVER. IT IS THE RAWEST, SWEETEST, UNINHIBITED AND EXQUISITE SOUNDS A PERSON CAN MAKE OR HEAR. IT ISN'T MUSIC, IT'S AN ENTIRE EXPERIENCE YOU FEEL AND LIVE. A SOUND TO RISE YOU UP AGAIN.

Amedée Ardoin
1896 – 1941

AMEDÉE ARDOIN WAS AN ACCORDIAN PLAYER FROM
SOUTH LOUISIANA IN THE FRENCH PART. HE PLAYED
AND SANG WITH THE SOUND AND THE VOICE AND THE
WORDS OF SOMETHING REALLY BROKEN UP INSIDE HIM
AND THE PEOPLE WHO LISTENED, LOVED HIM FOR THE
DEEP FEELING HE GAVE THEM. NOBODY COULD COPY
HOW HE PLAYED. NOBODY COULD DO WHAT HE DID ON
HIS INSTRUMENT. HE COULD MAKE UP SONGS RIGHT
WHILE HE WAS SINGING THEM. MOST OF THEM WERE
ABOUT HOW IT FEELS TO LEAVE A GIRL YOU LOVE,
TO LEAVE YOUR FAMILY, TO LEAVE YOUR HOME. HE
PLAYED AT WHITE DANCES AS WELL AS BLACK DANCES
WHICH WAS RARE FOR A BLACK MAN TO DO THERE,
AND ONE NIGHT AT A WHITE DANCE IT WAS HOT
AND A WOMAN HANDED AMEDÉE HER HANDKER-
CHIEF TO WIPE HIS FACE WITH AND THERE WERE
SOME PEOPLE THERE WHO DIDN'T LIKE THAT AND
THEY BEAT HIM SO BADLY THAT WHEN HIS BROTHER
FOUND HIM, AMEDÉE DIDN'T KNOW HIM OR ANYONE.
AFTER THAT, HIS MUSIC WAS GONE. HE DIED IN THE
LOUISIANA STATE INSTITUTION FOR THE MENTALLY ILL
ON NOVEMBER 4, 1941. IF YOU EVER GO, YOU WILL
STILL HEAR HIS SONGS BEING PLAYED. AT NIGHT
IN THE DANCEHALLS IN FRENCH LOUISIANA.

Iry Le Jeune
1928 — 1955

IRY LEJEUNE WAS A SWEET MAN WHO LOVED HIS WIFE AND CHILDREN AND WAS BORN TO A HARD WORKING TENANT FARMING FAMILY IN POINTE NOIRE, LOUISIANA. BECAUSE OF POOR EYESIGHT, HE COULDN'T WORK THE FIELDS SO HE SPENT HIS DAYS AT HIS COUSIN ANGELA'S HOUSE WHERE HE BEGAN TO LEARN THE ACCORDIAN AND LISTEN TO OLD RECORDINGS OF AMEDEE ARDOIN. IRY LOVED AMEDEE'S CRYING WAY OF SINGING AND PLAYING AND HE PRACTICED THIS STYLE UNTIL HE MADE IT HIS OWN, AND AFTER A TIME BECAME ONE OF THE BEST LOVED OF ALL CAJUN ACCORDIAN PLAYERS. HIS MUSIC CAPTURED ALL FEELINGS OF LONLINESS, HARDSHIP, AND ISOLATION THE PEOPLE OF HIS AREA KNEW. LISTENING TO HIM WOULD MAKE PEOPLE SHAKE WITH EMOTION. ONE NIGHT ON HIS WAY HOME FROM PLAYING A DANCE AT THE GREEN WING CLUB WITH FIDDLE PLAYER J.B. FUSELEIR, THEY GOT A FLAT TIRE AND AS THEY WERE FIXING IT, A PASSING CAR HIT IRY, KNOCKING HIM INTO A FIELD AND KILLING HIM INSTANTLY. HE WAS SURVIVED BY HIS WIFE WILMA AND HIS CHILDREN ERVIN, EDDIE, WILLIE BOY, EDWARD J. AND ELSIE MARIE.

Zodico Style

ALSO CALLED ZYDECO, ZORICO, ZORDICO, ZOLOGO, LA-LA.
ZODICO IS THE BLACK FRENCH STYLE OF MUSIC
FROM SOUTHWEST LOUISIANA. IT'S A MIX OF AFRO-
AMERICAN, FRENCH AFRO-CARIBBEAN AND CAJUN
STYLES AND IN THE PAST 25 YEARS INCLUDES
A LOT OF R+B AND SOUL INFLUENCES. IT IS
THE MUSIC OF THOSE WHO WERE ORIGINALLY
BROUGHT AS SLAVES FOR FRENCH PLANTERS IN THE
LATE 1700's, OR THE "GENS LIBRES DE COULEUR,"
BOTH BEFORE AND AFTER THE HATIAN REVOLUTION.
IT'S A FAST, WILDLY RHYTHMIC MUSIC USING
ACCORDIANS, FIDDLES AND THE VEST FROTTOIR, A
STEEL RUBBING BOARD WORN AND PLAYED WITH
SPOONS, BOTTLE OPENERS OR THIMBLES.- THE FROTTOIR
HAS IT'S ROOTS IN WEST AFRICAN AND CARIBBEAN
NOTCHED GOARDS SCRAPED TO GET A PARTICULAR
SOUND. WASHBOARDS WERE ORIGINALLY USED BEFORE
THE FROTTOIR. THE SINGING STYLES INCLUDE A
GOOD DEAL OF SPONTANEOUS YELLS, CHANTS AND
HUMOROUS LYRICS ABOUT DEACON JONES AND
UNCLE BUD. THERE ARE ALSO RIB CRACKING, SOUL
ACCENTED, SAD BLUES INFLUENCED SONGS THAT
CAPTURE EVERY POSSIBLE ANGLE ON HEARTBREAK.
IT'S THE ORIGINAL "GOOD TIME" MUSIC AND
"FEEL GOOD" MUSIC AND "BAD TIME" MUSIC AND
"FEEL BAD" MUSIC.

Cajun Style

CAJUN MUSIC COMES FROM THE WHITE FRENCH PEOPLE OF SOUTHWEST LOUISIANA WHO ARE DESCENDED FROM THE ACADIANS, A FARMING, FISHING AND TRAPPING PEOPLE WHO CAME FROM FRANCE, SETTLED IN NOVIA SCOTIA AND WERE DRIVEN FROM THEIR HOMES BY THE BRITISH IN 1764. THEY WENT SOUTH TO LOUISIANA WHERE THEY HELD ONTO THEIR LAND AND CULTURE BY FORMING TIGHT KNIT COMMUNITIES AND CREATING A BEAUTIFUL STYLE OF MUSIC. MUSIC BECAME THE FOCAL POINT OF NEARLY ALL SOCIAL GATHERINGS AND AN INTEGRAL PART OF CAJUN LIFE. THE SINGING STYLE IS FULL OF SUDDEN LOUD MOURNFUL WAILS AND LOUD FULL VOCALS BACKED BY FIDDLES AND ACCORDIANS AND A RHYTHM DRIVEN FORWARD ON A TRIANGLE AND DRUMS. CAJUN MUSIC CHANGED QUITE A BIT WITH THE INTRODUCTION OF AMPLIFICATION BUT IT STILL RETAINS THE BOLD SOUND OF PEOPLE WHO HAD TO MAKE THEMSELVES HEARD OVER BRAWLING CROWDS IN HOT DANCE HALLS. THERE IS A SADDER QUIETER SOUND TO CAJUN MUSIC AS WELL, THE SAD SONGS ARE EERIE AND LONLEY AND CAPTURE A CERTAIN SORT OF HARD ISOLATION THESE PEOPLE WERE FORCED TO MAINTAIN TO KEEP THEIR RICH CULTURE INTACT.

Cleoma Falcon
1905 - 1941

CLEOMA FALCON WAS A SMALL, ROUND WOMAN WITH CURLY BLACK HAIR, BLACK EYES, AND WHITE, WHITE SKIN. SHE PLAYED A LOUD, DRIVING, STEEL BODIED GUITAR WITH HER HUSBAND JOE, AN ACCORDIAN PLAYER. THEY PACKED DANCE HALLS THROUGHOUT SOUTHWEST LOUISIANA. THE SIGHT OF A WOMAN PLAYING IN A BAR SHOCKED THE PEOPLE OF THAT AREA AND THEY RODE IN BUGGIES FROM ALL OVER JUST TO HAVE A LOOK. THERE WAS NO VENTILATION AND THE COMBINATION OF DRINKING, DANCING AND THE SUFFOCATING HEAT WOULD MAKE PEOPLE FIGHT AND ACT WILD. CLEOMA AND JOE WOULD BE PROTECTED BY A SCREEN OF CHICKEN WIRE AROUND THE RAISED STAGE AND HAD TO PLAY LOUD ENOUGH TO BE HEARD OVER THE CROWD WHILE THEIR DAUGHTER LULU SLEPT ON A BLANKET IN THE CORNER. CLEOMA'S SINGING WAS FULL OF EMOTION AND COULD MAKE PEOPLE FEEL THE PAIN OF SEPARATION FROM THE ONES THEY LOVED. WHEN THEY RECORDED THE FIRST CAJUN RECORD MADE, "ALLONS à LAFAYETTE," PEOPLE COULDN'T BELIEVE ONE MAN AND ONE WOMAN COULD MAKE SUCH A SOUND. WHILE RETURNING FROM A RECORDING SESSION, CLEOMA'S JACKET WAS CAUGHT ON A PASSING VEHICAL AND SHE WAS DRAGGED THROUGH THE STREET. SHE WAS IN BAD HEALTH FROM THAT TIME UNTIL SHE DIED. AFTER SHE DIED, HER HUSBAND CONTINUED TO PLAY, BUT HIS FEELING FOR THE MUSIC HAD PASSED.

Blues Style

THE BLUES SOUND WAS BORN IN THE SOUTH FROM THE MUSIC OF THE BLACKS BROUGHT HERE AS SLAVES CARRYING WITH THEM AN EXPRESSIVE MUSICAL TRADITION THAT MET UP WITH AN INTOLERABLE WAY OF LIFE. AS GOSPEL MUSIC IS THE SOUND OF SOLACE THROUGH HOPE, BLUES IS THE SOUND OF SOLACE THROUGH THE EXPRESSION OF HOPELESSNESS, OF GIVING UP AND GIVING IN. IT'S A FEELING THAT MAKES A VERY SPECIFIC SOUND. THE COMMON THEMES OF BLUES SONGS ARE TRAVELING ACROSS LAND AND WATER, SEPARATION FROM LOVED ONES, BEING BROKE AND ALL OF THE SEVEN DEADLY SINS. IT'S BEEN CALLED "THE DEVIL'S MUSIC." BLUES CAN BE PLAYED ON ANYTHING FROM A BROOM WIRE STRUNG UP ON THE SIDE OF THE HOUSE AND RUBBED WITH AN OLD BOTTLE NECK TO B.B. KING'S FAMOUS "LUCILLE." A GOOD DESCRIPTION OF WHAT THE BLUES IS ABOUT COMES FROM JASPER LOVE: "I REMEMBER MY DADDY, HE WOULD CALL HISSELF SINGING ON THE BLUESSIDE. HE'D BE PLOUGHING THE MULE AND GET HOT AND YOU'D HEAR HIM OUT IN THE FIELD HOLLERING "I'M GOING UP THE BAYOU BABY AND I CAN'T CARRY YOU."

William Edward John
1937 — 1968
KNOWN AS "LITTLE WILLIE JOHN"

LITTLE WILLIE JOHN HAD ONE OF THE GREATEST VOICES OF ALL TIME. HE WAS BORN IN LAFAYETTE, ARKANSAS TO A MOTHER WHO PLAYED GOSPEL PIANO AND HE BEGAN SNEAKING OUT OF THE HOUSE AT THE AGE OF NINE TO SING ON THE STREETS AFTER HIS FAMILY MOVED TO DETROIT. WHEN HIS FATHER FOUND OUT HE GOT A WHIPPING. DIZZY GILLESPIE HEARD HIM SING AT A TALENT SHOW AND TALKED TO HIS PARENTS ABOUT HIS GREAT VOICE AND HIS PARENTS GAVE IN. AT 14 HE WAS SINGING WITH COUNT BASIE AND BY THE TIME HE WAS 20 HE HAD 20 TOP 20 R+B HITS. HIS VERSION OF "FEVER" BROKE RACIAL LINES AND MADE THE POP CHARTS WITH A SOUND THAT KNOCKED PEOPLE FLAT. HE HAD A REPUTATION FOR A BAD TEMPER, LYING, CHEATING, WILD SPENDING AND COULD CON PEOPLE OUT OF LOTS OF MONEY BY MAKING UP PITIFUL STORIES ABOUT HIS MOTHER. HE OFTEN CARRIED A KNIFE OR A GUN WHICH PEOPLE SAID HE DID BECAUSE HE WAS MAD ABOUT BEING SHORT. IN 1966 HE STABBED AND KILLED A MAN IN A CAFE BRAWL IN SEATTLE, WASHINGTON AND WENT TO THE WASHINGTON STATE PENITENTIARY WHERE HE DIED IN 1968. HIS DEATH CERTIFICATE SAYS THE CAUSE WAS A HEART ATTACK, OTHERS SAY HE WAS BEATEN AND DIED DURING AN OPERATION TO RELIEVE PRESSURE ON HIS BRAIN.

Hociel Thomas
1904 - 1952

HOCIEL THOMAS WAS BORN IN HOUSTON, TEXAS
TO A FAMILY WITH ROOTS IN CHURCH MUSIC.
HER GRANDFATHER WAS A DEACON AT THE SHILOH
BAPTIST CHURCH AND HER FATHER WAS A MUSI-
CIAN AND SONG WRITER. WHEN SHE WAS 12
YEARS OLD SHE WAS SENT TO LIVE WITH HER
AUNT, SIPPIE WALLACE IN NEW ORLEANS. THERE
WASN'T A BETTER TIME TO BE LEARNING TO PLAY
PIANO THAN NEW ORLEANS IN THE TWENTIES AND
TOGETHER WITH HER AUNT SHE WORKED HOUSE
PARTIES, NIGHT CLUBS AND STORIEVILLE HOUSES
WHEN PIANO PLAYERS WERE THE MAIN SOURCE
OF MUSICAL ENTERTAINMENT. WHEN SHE WAS
20 SHE MOVED TO CHICAGO AND WORKED WITH
LOUIS ARMSTRONG AND OTHERS. SHE MARRIED
ARTHUR TEBO AND THEY HAD A DAUGHTER WHO
WAS LATER SENT TO NEW ORLEANS AND ALSO
RAISED BY SIPPIE WALLACE. HOCIELS VOICE
ALWAYS KEPT THE MAJESTY OF CHURCH SINGING
WHICH MAKES FOR A POWERFUL SOUND WHEN
COMBINED WITH NEW ORLEANS STYLE BLUES PIANO
SHE MOVED TO OAKLAND AND ONE NIGHT SHE AND
HER SISTER GOT INTO A FIGHT WHERE HOCIEL'S
EYES WERE PUT OUT AND HER SISTER WAS KILLED
SHE WAS TRIED AND ACQUITTED OF MANSLAUGHTER,
STOPPED PLAYING MUSIC AND LATER DIED OF
HEART DISEASE. SHE'S BURIED IN GREENLAWN
CEMETARY IN SAN FRANCISCO.

Country Style

EARLY COUNTRY MUSIC IS THE SOUND OF THE WHITE SOUTHERN WORKING PEOPLE. IT'S A REGIONAL FARM STYLE SOUND THAT DEVELOPED IN DIFFERENT WAYS IN LITTLE POCKETS AND COMMUNITIES THROUGHOUT THE SOUTH, EVOLVING PRIMARILY OUT OF A RESERVOIR OF FOLK SONGS, BALLADS, AND INSTRUMENTAL PIECES BROUGHT TO NORTH AMERICA BY ANGLO-CELTIC IMMIGRANTS. ALTHOUGH IT IS A "WHITE SOUND" IT ABSORBED MANY INFLUENCES FROM BLACK CULTURE IN TERMS OF SPIRITUALS, BLUES, RAGTIME, R+B AND VOCALIZATION AND INSTRUMENTAL STYLES. EVEN TODAY IT IS COMMON FOR A BLACK SONG TO BE COVERED BY A WHITE C+W SINGER AND BECOME A HIT. A WIDE VARIETY OF MUSICAL STYLES FALL INTO THE CLASSIFICATION OF "COUNTRY" FROM FRAIL ODD SINGING TO THE BAREST ACCOMPANIMENT TO STUNNING HARMONIES THAT ARE PRECISE AND HAUNTING WITH MUSIC THAT IS PLAYED SO PRECISELY AND QUICKLY IT'S LIKE HITTING THE GAS AND THE BRAKES AT THE SAME TIME BUT IN A GORGEOUS WAY. THE COMMON THEMES OF COUNTRY MUSIC ARE TRUE LOVE, FAMILY, DRINKING, TRUCKS, HARD WORK, ADULTERY, WILD LIVING, RELIGIOUS REMORSE AND MY WOMAN DON'T UNDERSTAND ME.

Arthur Phelps
1890-5? — 1930?

ARTHUR PHELPS WAS BORN MAYBE IN JACKSONVILLE, FLORIDA AND MAYBE NOT BECAUSE NO ONE REALLY KNOWS. HE WANDERED THROUGHOUT THE SOUTH DRINKING WHISKEY AND GOING BY THE NAMES OF BLIND BLAKE, BLIND ARTHUR, BILLY JAMES, GORGEOUS WEED, BLIND GEORGE MARTIN AND OTHERS. HE HOBOED AND SANG FOR ROAD GANGS, PICNICS, HOUSE PARTIES, FISH FRIES AND ANYWHERE WHERE PEOPLE NEEDED TO HEAR MUSIC. HE PLAYED A CLEAN BLUES AND RAGTIME GUITAR WHICH HE LIKED TO HOLD UP BEHIND HIS HEAD AND PLAY FAST AND SMOOTH. IN THE MID-TWENTIES HE WORKED HIS WAY UP TO CHICAGO, MADE SOME RECORDINGS, AND MOVED INTO A PLACE ON 31st STREET AND COTTAGE GROVE AVENUE. HIS APARTMENT WAS A POPULAR SPOT FOR MUSICIANS TO COME AND PRACTICE AND DRINK MOONSHINE. ONE DAY HE DISAPPEARED. AFTER 1930 NO ONE SAW HIM AGAIN. SOME SAY HE GOT HIT BY A STREET CAR, OTHERS SAY HE JUST HEADED SOUTH.

Girl Groups

ONCE ONLY HEARD AS HEATED BACK-UP VOCALISTS, THE GIRL GROUPS OF THE LATE 50's AND EARLY 60's CAME ONTO THE SCENE DURING A TIME WHEN BLACK POPULAR MUSIC WAS MAKING ITS ROUGH TRANSITION FROM SMOOTH R+B TO RAW "BLACK IS BEAUTIFUL" SOUL SCREAMING. MOST OF THESE GROUPS WERE VERY YOUNG AND HAD AN ALMOST NAIVE EN-THUSIASTIC SHOUT/SINGING STYLE THAT CONVEYED A LOT OF POWER AND EMOTION UNTIL SEVERAL MAJOR LABELS GOT A HOLD OF IT. BECAUSE THIS SOUND PROVED TO HAVE A LOT OF CROSS-OVER POTENTIAL, THE GROUPS THAT "MADE IT" DID SO BY HAVING THEIR AUTHENTIC GRITTY STYLE CARE-FULLY WRUNG OUT BY THE STRICT, SUFFOCATING MANAGEMENT OF MEN SUCH AS PHIL SPECTOR AND BERRY GORDY WHO MADE EVERY DECISION FOR THEM WITH AN EYE ON CREATING MAINSTREAM SUCCESS. THESE MANAGERS CREATED A SPECIFIC INNOCUOUS SOUND AND THE WOMEN WITHIN THE GROUPS BECAME INTERCHANGEABLE. SAYS BEVERLY LEE OF THE SHIRELLES "I ALWAYS THOUGHT OUR SONGS WERE CORNEY AND LOLLIPOPISH. WE WERE MIDDLE OF THE ROAD BUT PEOPLE LIKED IT." MOST OF THESE GROUPS HAD ONLY ONE HIT, WHICH WAS NOT DUE TO A LACK OF TALENT BUT RATHER DUE TO A SPECIFIC MACHINE OF MANAGEMENT REQUIRED TO STRIP DOWN THE SOUND AND MAKE IT FIT IN WITH WHAT WAS CONSIDERED PROFITABLE. THANKS TO THIS SORT OF ORGANIZATION, THE GIRL GROUPS' SOUND WENT FROM A VROOMING 100MPH SOUND OF THE IKETTES SINGING "I'M BLUE" TO THE WASHED OUT ZERO MPH SOUND OF THE LAST SUPREMES' HITS IN A FEW SHORT YEARS.

R. H. (REBERT) HARRIS
b. 1909
"THE FATHER OF THEM ALL"

R.H. HARRIS HAS BEEN CREDITED WITH ALMOST SINGLE HANDEDLY REVOLUTIONIZING NOT ONLY BLACK GOSPEL MUSIC BUT SECULAR SOUL MUSIC AS WELL. BY CREATING A SINGING STYLE WHICH HAS BEEN DESCRIBED AS "SWEET, MANLY AND TERRIFYING" AND WEAVING IT IN AND OUT OF CLOSE CHANTING FOUR PART BACK UP HARMONIES, THIS MAN CAUSED CHURCH WOMEN TO HAVE UNCONTROLLABLE FITS. HE SAYS HE LEARNED HIS ELECTRIFYING VOCAL STYLE FROM IMITATING BIRDS ON THE SMALL TEXAS FARM WHERE HE GREW UP AND THIS PASSIONATE SOUND CAN BE HEARD IN SAM COOKE'S SINGING BE-CAUSE R.H. HARRIS TAUGHT SAM COOKE TO SING. WHEN HARRIS'S QUINTET, THE SOUL STIRRERS, BE-CAME SO POPULAR THAT WOMEN WERE CLIMBING ALL OVER THEM AND "THE GROUP'S MORALS FELL RIGHT INTO THE WATER" HARRIS, A VERY RELIGIOUS MAN, STEPPED DOWN AND SAM COOKE TOOK HIS PLACE, IMITATING HARRIS AS BEST HE COULD. WHEN COOKE SHOCKED THE GOSPEL WORLD BY CROSSING OVER, HE CARRIED WITH HIM EVERY ONE OF HARRIS' INNOVATIONS AND EVER AFTER THE WORLD OF BLACK POPULAR MUSIC HAS BEEN SHOT THROUGH WITH HARRIS' INFLUENCE. IF SAM COOKE IS THE FATHER OF SWEET SOUL SINGING, R.H. HARRIS IS THE FATHER'S FATHER. THE FATHER OF THEM ALL.

La Verne Lois Williamson
b. JULY 9 1923 iN Pike COUNTY Kentucky

LA VERNE WILLIAMSON WAS BORN TO A COALMINING
FATHER AND A HARD WORKING MOTHER IN MC VEIGH,
KENTUCKY. SHE SAID HER TOWN WAS SO SMALL
"YOU HAD TO BREAK DAYLIGHT WITH A SLEDGE HAM-
MER AND THE GROUND HOGS CARRIED IN THE MAIL."
SHE SANG AND PLAYED THE GUITAR AND CHANGED HER
NAME TO MOUNTAIN FERN, DIXIE LEE, AND THEN
SETTLED ON MOLLY O'DAY. PEOPLE CALLED HER THE
FEMALE ROY ACUFF. IN 1942 AFTER HER
MARRIAGE TO LYNN DAVIS, SHE STARTED SINGING
COUNTRY GOSPEL AND MADE HITS WITH SONGS
LIKE "MATTHEW 24", "TRAMP ON THE STREET,"
AND "DON'T SELL DADDY ANYMORE WHISKEY."
NO FEMALE COUNTRY SINGER WAS MORE POPULAR
IN THE 40's THAN MOLLY O'DAY. IN 1952 SHE
GOT TUBERCULOSIS AND HAD PART OF HER LUNG
REMOVED. AFTER A LONG TIME OF BEING SICK,
SHE RECOVERED AND SPENT LESS TIME ON MUSIC
AND MORE TIME ON RELIGION. HER HUSBAND
BECAME A MINISTER IN THE CHURCH OF GOD
AND THEY PASTORED TOGETHER AT DIFFERENT
CHURCHES. IN 1962 THEY OPENED A GOSPEL
RECORD STORE IN HUNT WEST VIRGINIA WHERE
LYNN GOT A JOB AT AN INVESTMENT FIRM.
SHE CONTINUED TO PREACH AT REVIVALS WHEN-
EVER HER HEALTH PERMITTED.

Otis Redding
1941 — 1967

OTIS REDDING GREW UP IN A HOUSING PROJECT IN MACON, GEORGIA KNOWN AS BELLEVUE BUT CALLED "HELL VIEW" BY IT'S RESIDENTS. BOTH LITTLE RICHARD AND JAMES BROWN WERE RUNNING WILD THROUGH THE TOWN AT THE TIME AND OTIS WOULD SEE THEM PERFORM AND SAY "ONE OF THESE DAYS, I'M GOING TO BE JUST LIKE THEM." HE QUIT SCHOOL IN THE 10TH GRADE AND TURNED EVERY MINUTE TOWARD MUSIC. LIKE MOST R+B SINGERS, OTIS GOT HIS START IN THE CHURCH WHERE ROUGH, DEEP, PASSIONATE SINGING MOVED CONGREGATIONS THE WAY OTIS WAS EVENTUALLY ABLE TO MOVE THE WORLD WITH HIS MOURNFUL SWEET VOCALS. HIS BIG BREAK CAME WHEN THERE WAS A HALF AN HOUR LEFT DURING A STAX RECORDING SESSION WHERE OTIS WAS WORKING WITH A GROUP CALLED JOHNNY JENKINS AND THE PINETOPPERS. SOMEONE SUGGESTED OTIS TRY SOMETHING ON HIS OWN AND THE RESULT WAS THE HAUNTING "THESE ARMS OF MINE" WHICH WAS RELEASED IN 1962. NO ONE COULD SING WITH THE KIND OF ACHING LOVE PAIN OTIS PUT OUT, A STYLE OF SINGING THAT EARNED HIM THE NAME OF MR. PITIFUL. HE PLAYED THE APOLLO IN 1963 AND THE REST, AS THEY SAY, IS HISTORY. ON DECEMBER 9TH 1967, HE WAS KILLED IN A PLANE CRASH. IN MARCH OF 1968, HIS RECORDING OF "DOCK OF THE BAY" HIT NUMBER ONE.

◉ *List of Paintings*

 Bibliography

Adventures of a Ballad Hunter
Lomax, John
New York, MacMillan Co. 1947

Blues Fell This Morning
Oliver, Paul
New York, Horizon Press 1960

Blues People
Jones, LeRoi
New York, William Morrow and Company 1963

Blues Who's Who
Harris, Sheldon
New York, De Capo Press, Inc. 1979

Cajun Music: A Reflection of a People
Savoy, Ann Allen
Eunice, Louisiana, Bluebird Press, Inc. 1984

The Country Music Story
Shelton, Robert
Indianapolis, The Bobbs-Merril Co. 1966

Country Music USA
Malone, Bill
Austin, University of Texas Press 1968

The Encyclopedia of Folk, Country and Western Music
Stambler, Irwin and Grelun, Landon
New York, St. Martin 1969

Feel Like Going Home
Guralnick, Peter
New York, Vintage 1981

The Gospel Sound
Heilbut, Anthony
New York, Limelight Edition 1985

I Hear You Knockin'
Hannush, Jeff
Ville Platte, LA. Swallow Publications 1985

Lost Highway
Guralnick, Peter
New York, Vintage 1979

The Nashville Sound
Hempel, Paul
New York, Simon and Schuster 1970

Rock Archives
Ochs, Michael
New York, Dolphin 1984

Showtime at the Apollo
Ted Fox
New York, Holt, Rinehart and Winston 1983

Sweet Soul Music
Guralnick, Peter
New York, Harper and Row 1986

Also by Lynda Barry

GIRLS + BOYS
BIG IDEAS
NAKED LADIES! NAKED LADIES! NAKED LADIES!